Mother California

Atlas & Co.
New York

Mother California

A Story of Redemption Behind Bars

Kenneth E. Hartman

Atlas & Co. *Publishers*
15 West 26th Street, 2nd floor
New York, NY 10010
www.atlasandco.com

Distributed to the trade by W. W. Norton & Company

Printed in the United States

Atlas & Company books may be purchased for educational, business, or sales promotional use. For information, please write to info@atlasandco.com.

Library of Congress Cataloging-in-Publication Data is available upon request.

ISBN: 978-1-934633-19-9
13 12 11 10 09 1 2 3 4 5 6

For Alia Marie, my beloved daughter,
the one purely good thing in my life.
You freed me in the most important ways.
I am proud to be your father.
I will always love you.

North Long Beach

When I was nineteen, I killed a man in a drunken, drugged-up fistfight.

Anyone who knew me could have seen it coming. I had spent my entire adolescence in and out of major trouble. I stole, I lied, I cheated. I was extraordinarily, preternaturally violent. In my short life, I had left behind me a pile of wreckage. I was, in the euphemism of the outcast, "state-raised," a child of Mother California. In my world, it's a title to be proud of; surviving an upbringing in the Golden State's juvenile prison system is considered something of an accomplishment.

Before I was eligible for a driver's license, I had witnessed stabbings and beatings too numerous to count, and I had participated in more than I care to recall. I had seen boys gang-rape other boys in the shower. I had beaten others unconscious simply because of a misspoken word. On one occasion, in Orange County Juvenile Hall, when I was fifteen, after fighting with ten guards, I spent days naked in a rubber-walled room with a hole in the floor. Stripped to the bare necessities, one learns that respect is to be demanded at all costs, on penalty of death, even one's own.

In every jail and juvenile camp I learned the same lesson. No one ever wanted to know what I did for a living; they wanted to see if I was predator or prey. Shoved against a wall, surrounded in a dark alley, looking into the barrel of a battered service revolver, I always got the same message: Will you stand up and fight, or will you bow down? The winnowing process began on the schoolyard and ended with only the baddest of the badasses still standing.

It became a job, this posture of hardness. Like the time the local girls came to me and said some guy had disrespected them in our neighborhood. Though I considered them little more than receptacles in tight pants, I ran to their defense. He was a fellow predator, I recognized instantly. The torn jeans, the dusty combat boots, the jangling keys hanging off his leather belt, all of these marked him as another sidewalk commando. More to the point, the deadened hardness around his reddened eyes identified him as a citizen of my world. I walked up to him and demanded he apologize. He leaned back and patted the side of his shirt. "I'm packing," he told me, the outlines of the pistol's butt visible. I stepped closer and told him to either start shooting or start apologizing. He looked into my eyes and saw an inflexible fearlessness, an irrational aggression. After he made his act of contrition, he walked away, tossing over his shoulder, "You're fucking crazy." It was a grudging compliment. This was who I was; this was who I aspired to be.

It all imploded one February night in 1980 when I encountered poor Thomas Allen Fellowes. I had spent the night in a series of bars, the kind of bars frequented by men with tattooed necks and women drawn to chaos and rampant testosterone. I was fresh out of my latest stint in Mother California's Youth Authority, known to all of us who had walked her unforgiving yards as the Y.A. Two hundred and twenty pounds, six foot two, a coiled spring of hostility, I had the dead eyes familiar to prison guards and combat veterans. I walked with the studied indifference of the fearless, although my impetus was, on deeper reflection from this distant vantage, undistilled fear: fear of the other, fear that I would be discovered to be weaker than my act. Deeper still, down beyond my casual, bruised comprehension, I was desperately lonely and sad.

That February night, in the last couple of hours before closing time at The Honey Bee bar, I had achieved the level of inebriation at which one becomes, functionally, a kind of demigod. I was fully alert and coherent, a product of massive doses of prescription methedrine, while at the same time blind drunk on tequila. I was on an undefeated arm-wrestling run. The very fine barmaid kept telling me to hang around till she got off with barely disguised promises of carnal pleasures. I had already received a knee-buckling blowjob from some strange girl in the parking lot. The night had been perfect, but for the lack of real violence.

In pursuit of calamity, I managed to persuade some men from The Honey Bee to make a run over to the local shit-kicker tavern. A dozen of us piled into a van and crashed the other bar. Tattooed necks and big belt buckles never get along, even in the best of circumstances. After a traditional exchange of epithets, the fight took off. Now I had entered my zone, my place of comfort. Mock battles and feats of strength never really satisfied me. I needed to feel the crunch of knuckles on bone, see the blood spray out from the point of impact, hear the grunts and groans of pain, smell the tang of fear in the air as I whaled away. In those moments of actual combat, I was transfigured; I lost my contact with the dull earth, and ascended to the rarified realms of beasts and legends. By the time we got back to The Honey Bee, after I had knocked somebody's teeth out and stood roaring my defiance and exhilaration amid a barrage of beer bottles, I was a champion, but I also saw the dawning recognition in my companions' bloodshot eyes. They realized a monster was in their midst.

We golems of urban legend were a force field of the darkest energy. I had gotten to the point where I could feel the fear I brought out in people. When I walked in the front door of parties, others ran out the back door. Beyond the thrill-seeking women and danger junkies who periodically hitched a ride in my wake, people sensed the blackness and avoided me. There was so little humanity alive in me, so little good. Rage at the nature of existence was all I knew.

I left The Honey Bee with my friend Bob in his beat-up Pontiac station wagon. Bob, whose own personal tragedies had hollowed him out, didn't fear me, even at my worst. He was six foot four, with a voice that rumbled down in the lowest register, a calm basso profundo. His shining black hair

framed an equally Irish and Japanese face. In all the years I'd
known him, going back to elementary school, he had always
projected solidity. We would be totally smashed, rampaging
on a cocktail of drugs, and he would still seem together.
His calm demeanor masked a childhood so horrendous it
was only spoken of when he wasn't around, and always in
hushed and sympathetic tones. He had suffered too many
beatings, too many public humiliations at the hands of his
drunken father. We drove down the 91 Freeway, slipping
back into the underbelly of South Los Angeles, back to our
little shit-hole neighborhood of Northtown, on the seedy
edge of Long Beach. The Eagles played on the radio. The
road was clear and devoid of cops as we sped on to the few
moments that would define the rest of my life.

I decided to check the park for any stray girls looking for a
place to crash. They could often be found wandering around
in the chill night air trying to stay warm. On some winter
nights in Southern California there is a mist that forms
halos around the streetlights. That night the air was damp
and cool, wet with the ocean. I reached into my pocket for
a smoke, lit up, and blew smoke rings into the night air.

Turning the corner in the dark, I saw a shape lying on one
of the picnic tables. On closer inspection, the shape proved
to be a man asleep with his shoes off. I slapped the soles of
his feet and demanded to know why he was sleeping in my
park. He jumped up, startled but game, and informed me it
was none of my goddamned business. I suggested he had best
tell me or I'd kick his ass. Up to this point we were dancing
a little two-step—a verbal joust without much weight. Mr.
Fellowes proved he wasn't state-raised when he said to an

obviously drunk, much larger phantom in the middle of the night, "You aren't going to do anything, you punk."

He called me a punk. Me, the unbeatable giant of the neighborhood. In my park I was being called a punk. In addition to its other less-than-flattering connotations, a punk in juvenile jails in California is a boy that other boys screw in the ass.

I swung on him in a big, arching left hook that failed to connect with anything. Now I was doubly mad. I swung again and managed to connect. In the next thirty seconds, I reduced Mr. Fellowes to a bleeding lump on the concrete. The coroner would testify that he was probably dead after the first punch. But I wasn't satisfied, so I kicked him in a blur of energy until I'd spent my fury on his unconscious body. Before I left, I threw all his property around the park—up on the roof of the public restroom, out on the grass—on the assumption that he was merely knocked out. I wanted him to have to scramble to recover his belongings just as I had to recover my sense of pride. I was no punk.

*

It took them less than twenty-four hours to find me.

Around 3:00 a.m. the next night, Bob and I were driving around aimlessly, realizing in the same corner of our minds that we were through. We noticed a lone detective's car pull in behind us, its flasher off, tailing us for a few miles. We debated our strategy and settled on heading over to Bellflower, down Oak Street, where we would try pulling into a long driveway and jump out of the car in different directions. Just as we pulled onto Bellflower Boulevard we saw an armada of Long Beach Police cars pouring off the 91 Freeway. They fanned out across the road as the detectives behind us finally turned on the flashing lights. By then we were surrounded. A loudspeaker ordered us to place our hands on the dashboard. In a few seconds, a blur of blue uniforms converged on us. I could hear a metallic clicking against the passenger door window to my right. I glanced that way to see the barrel of a pump shotgun nervously skittering, held by a young woman whose eyes looked more terrified than any I had ever seen.

Bob ended up in the back of one car and I in another. On the ride downtown one of the detectives was joshing with his partner, asking if he had a crystal ball; how else could they have tracked me down so fast? The crime had occurred less than twenty-four hours before. It was no crystal ball; my own homeboys had turned me in. I only learned this later, but I wasn't surprised. I never developed any close friendships in my neighborhood. Instead, I had managed to antagonize any number of pretend tough guys who weren't prepared to deal with a son of Mother California's prison training camps. In the brief seventy-three days of my latest bout of freedom I had kicked down a few doors, beaten several guys into unconsciousness, and unnerved everyone around me. Street toughs are formidable, but inside toughs—guys who've served time—are a whole different level of dangerous.

While I was being processed into the city jail, one of the older jailers put a young rookie on the search detail. About halfway into the process, the jailer told him I was being booked for beating someone to death. The blanching of the skin, the curious way fear dilates pupils, the slight drawing away: I saw all of this for the first time. I felt a surge of power run through me. I had reached the pinnacle of antisocial behavior; I had killed with my bare hands. My foot still ached from where I had stomped on a man's head. My knuckles were scraped from that episode and several other fistfights I'd gotten into the night before. Yet I felt no shame, no guilt, nothing. I was in a jail being booked for murder, scaring the police, and I felt nothing.

That first night in the city jail, one of the jailers made the mistake of venturing too far into the cell area and got beaten up pretty bad. He lay there on the floor for quite some time before one of his peers discovered him. Half an hour later the guy who had attacked him was dragged out by a small army of police. A while later he returned, tossed into the block like a bloody bag.

I was crammed into a tiny cell with three other guys, all in for violent crimes of one kind or another. The beds were so close together that I could hardly squeeze through to the back of the cell to the toilet. I hoisted myself up onto one of the upper bunks and lit a cigarette. Ten minutes later I was sleeping my normal, dreamless sleep.

Every jail has its quirks, its special forms of cruelty. The Long Beach City Jail was no different. Every morning we were ordered out of the cells into a common area with metal tables that had little round metal seats welded to them. The walls were blank. We were forced to stay in this featureless room until late at night. The food was about jail normal, which meant it had no discernible taste and the consistency of wet mush. Jail food is cooked until there is no more taste; no spices are used, no efforts made to enhance flavor. It is dead food. There were no showers, no phones, no normal human amenities to speak of. It was designed and run, like all such places, to break you down.

My first priority was to figure out how to steal more food and get more smokes. The jail trustee was an old white guy with bad tattoos and broken teeth, a pack of smokes rolled up in his shirtsleeve. I jammed him up at the first opportunity and appealed to our only real commonality: race. By the end of the day, I had secured a second tray and a pack of Camels.

The police detectives called me in for the requisite interview. I told them I had nothing to say. The older one advised me they didn't beat confessions out of suspects anymore. He looked wistful: life had gotten so complicated. By the next day, I was on a sheriff's bus to the Men's Central Jail.

Los Angeles County Jail: I

Within the California penal system, Los Angeles County Jail is held in high esteem for its capacity to induce terror. There's no other jail like it. Ten thousand men crammed into a small bunker of a building, a pile of unpainted concrete. Like all new arrivals, I'm packed into a large, windowless room with a hundred others from all over the county. After hours of stifling closeness, a pack of deputies pours into the room and orders everyone to stand around the perimeter. Thus begins the infamous group strip search—welcome to the county jail, you who do not have the means to bail out. In a series of barked commands, everyone is told to get naked, with their worldly possessions piled in front of them. The deputies have performed this routine so many times they've lost interest. One old, naked black man, unable to keep up the pace, is directed to the center of the room and told to dance. Remarkably, he begins to shuffle his feet and dance. We shake out our underwear, bang our shoes together, bend over and spread our ass cheeks and cough. We then pick up our clothes and head into another room for hours more of waiting. When we gain access to pay phones, I have no one to call. The only strong admonition my father ever gave me after I turned eighteen—"Stay away from that goddamned park"—I had failed to heed. There wasn't much more to talk about.

*

There's a saying amongst county jail habitués: "It's on like 9000." This is because 9000 is the first module you're packed into after being processed, after being issued jail clothes, after the delousing shower, after the twenty-four or forty-eight or seventy-two hours it takes to make it through the booking front, the mug shots, the fingerprinting, the wristband being affixed with the simple advice, "Get caught without this and we'll kick your ass." It is a huge open-bay dorm crammed with bunk beds. It's the introduction to the county jail experience.

On that first night, a young white boy, looking a little too feminine perhaps, is gang-raped in the back of the dorm—a dozen angry blacks variously beating and sodomizing him, sometimes at the same time. Fights break out constantly. The deputies remain safely ensconced in a glassed-in booth, far from the action. I'm reminded right then that any fight is a life-or-death proposition; any challenge must be met with an instantaneous, violent response. I also learn that in this hellhole being part of a tiny, hated minority makes it a vital necessity to band together with those who will stand up for us. Every morning, as we're herded out to breakfast, the casualties stagger from their cells and beg for protection from the deputies.

Periodically, the deputies rush into the dorm in a phalanx, armed with their ever-present foot-and-a-half-long flashlights and a brutal determination to extract some pain. Everyone in the dorm is stripped naked, more bending and spreading and coughing, as all the bunks are tossed. Inevitably, at least one prisoner will say the wrong thing or display a demeanor the deputies find offensive. Almost always this is one of the blacks, who ends up being dragged out and beaten down. He'll return later, lumped up and heroic.

Thus far, I've managed to stay out of the mix. But 9000 is a way station, so I'm transferred out to 2200, second floor, old side, one of the high modules. Walking down the tier with my bedroll, I'm greeted with, "Another one of those fucking Nazis, cuz." To many of the young blacks, all whites are Nazis. The next morning a welcoming party of blacks stands outside my cell, ready to rush in together and rat pack me. I know I'm about to get the crap beaten out of me, but I also know there's no option but to fight or die—or worse, be sodomized. As the cell door is opening, an older black guy in my cell, Floyd Thomas, jumps in front of me and tells the wrecking crew they can come in one at a time, since I'm obviously willing to fight, or else he's going to back my play. It's an excruciatingly awkward moment.

*

The white-black divide in California jails in 1980 was just as violent as it was in '50s-era Mississippi. The population breakdown in the high modules, where the violent criminals were held, ran about twelve blacks to every white. It didn't help that the deputy sheriffs tended to look a lot more like me than the vast, pissed-off majority of prisoners. Nor did it help that those same deputies were notorious for beating their mostly black charges into bloody pulp for sport. A well-earned reputation, I learned early on.

Floyd's presence ensured my cell would be a relatively safe haven—I only got into two fistfights in our six-man cell. Out and about was a wholly different matter. For the duration of my five-month stay, I fought at least a couple of times a week, sometimes a couple of times in the same day. It all boiled down to the simple black-white issue. More than three hundred years of fury unleashed inside the pressure cooker confines of the county jail. Several times, as I was walking out to chow with a fresh shiner or a fat lip, the deputies would ask me if I wanted to move to one of the single-cell modules. I always took offense at this and refused. Although the hatred didn't lessen, I suspect my antagonists came to have a grudging respect for my tenacity, if nothing else. When dope came on the tier, someone would come by and slide me a joint. More than once, when a new softy was being passed around, I was invited to the party, lust trumping bloodlust.

The indignities of the county jail were almost unbelievable, even to me. I once stood, naked, nose to the wall, for a full eight-hour shift because a young deputy didn't think my tone deferential enough. On another occasion, when I was again naked and on a wall, an older deputy—performing his training duties, I suppose—calmly explained to a younger one that my tattoos were a clear indication I was "a piece of shit." In most jails and prisons the guards will at least make a pretense of treating the prisoners with a modicum of respect, a crumb of courtesy. Not so in Los Angeles County Jail. And this rabid violence and disdain fed all the outrages we prisoners committed against each other. The vicious cycle went round and round; we all hung on as best we could.

*

The day I'm to be tried for killing Mr. Fellowes starts like any other court run: At 3:00 a.m., we're packed into one of the innumerable holding cages down on the first floor, in the back of the jail. I can hear the fleet of big black-and-white buses warming up their diesel engines; the smell of exhaust is heavy in the air. Deputy sheriffs are everywhere, clutching printouts of names for each of the various courthouses scattered throughout Los Angeles County. After we're identified by our wristbands, hand-cuffed onto one of the four corners of a restraint chain, and loaded onto the bus for our specific destination, the buses pull out in a cloud of belching smoke. We bounce down the Long Beach freeway, carried along in the crush of early morning traffic. From my seat ten feet above the asphalt I can see down into the cars, the beautiful young women in their short skirts, the harried men in their tight ties, the world on its way to work. Most disconcerting are the school buses that pull up alongside. The children are curious; sometimes they wave, other times they stick their tongues out, or turn away.

After sitting in a holding tank for a couple of hours, I'm escorted into the courtroom. A small group of potential jurors, mostly older folks, is seated behind the prosecutor's table. Jury selection begins and ends in short order. Then the prosecutor gives his opening statement, announcing that the people are not seeking the death penalty. In his ill-fitting, rumpled plaid suit, he is a lawyer version of a pilot—reassuring, down-to-earth, competent without being flashy. Speaking in a Southern drawl, he launches into a devastating attack on me. The jury is mesmerized. My public defender gives his opening. After the prosecutor's brutal eloquence, his bored recitation seems flat and ineffective. The jury looks unimpressed.

The witnesses take the stand. A girl I gave a ride to out of pity describes how a homeboy told her the names of the two boys who happened upon the scene that night. I had jacked them against a wall and told them to spin in the other direction. In their testimony this is transformed into me attempting to rob them. The police detective testifies. The coroner provides a slew of horrifying color photographs of the victim in different states of dissection. The jury is obviously repulsed. I'm shocked myself. The last time I saw this man he was facedown on the concrete, unconscious and immobile. He wasn't naked, and his organs weren't on display. The prosecutor takes a long time discussing each photo, looking sidelong at the jurors, an apologetic expression on his face, and then turns back with grim resolve. The people rest its case.

All eyes in the courtroom turn to the defense. I take the stand. My public defender invites me to tell the jury my side of the story. It's pretty basic: I happened upon the victim, accosted him, and then antagonized him until a fight broke out. The prosecutor cross-examines me for a solid hour, asking me the same questions a dozen different ways. It doesn't go well. He's a man on fire. Practiced at the art of outrage, he stalks the courtroom, flaying me with open contempt, his voice rising and falling, mocking, accusing. I'm a stand-in for all that is evil and wrong with society—not merely the murderer of Mr. Fellowes, but murder itself, sitting right there in their midst. I must be stopped or they'll be in peril. My attempts to explain how it all started when Mr. Fellowes called me a punk are met with incredulous stares. I'm from a different world, a world without courts and lawyers, a world incomprehensible to those not of it.

My public defender's closing argument is a recitation of the facts. He obviously couldn't care less about the outcome, one way or the other. Not once during the trial does he shake my hand or display any kind of human connection. The jury is then given four hours of instructions. They retire to a private room to deliberate. No one doubts the outcome, although the speed of their decision surprises everyone. Two hours later, I'm back in court, found guilty on all counts—

murder, attempted robbery, and the special circumstance of killing in the commission of a crime, attempted robbery, inherently dangerous to human life. The entire process—from motions to jury selection, to opening statements, the people's case, the defendant's case, to closing arguments, to verdict—takes less than two days. The sentence, meted out a month later, is life without the possibility of parole. The other death penalty.

Poor Bob, whose crime boiled down to picking his friends with an appalling lack of good judgment, ultimately received a life with parole sentence. To my knowledge, he remains in prison. That was twenty-nine years and several lifetimes ago. I have never spoken again with any of my siblings, and my parents are both dead. I have never seen any of the people I knew then. It's as if I've been sentenced to death by a very long and protracted method, one that includes the gradual imposition of a civil and social death, a sort of dematerialization—as if the life I led before prison was a dream, and the life I lead now the only reality.

Reception-Guidance Center, Chino

The holding tank is crowded and there's a heady mix of anticipation and fear in the air. It's 5:00 a.m. and we've been waiting here since 3:00 a.m., maybe all our lives, to catch the chain to the joint. (That's what it was called back then, "catching the chain." I've never figured out how it came to be called this, but the ominous quality of the phrase sounded perfect to my ear.) I'm headed for the California Institution for Men at Chino.

Five months in the Los Angeles County Jail have hardened me. When I ask some tough, older ex-con how tough prison really is, he tells me I've already done time in the toughest prison in the state. But I'm nervous anyway. The "joint"—a state prison, not a mere jail—just isn't a very good place to be. Add to this the fact that prisoners love to tell so-very-tall tales of how rough the place was they just left or were slated to be going. Terrible as the county jail was, after my five months of combat I have come to grips with its realities. Fear of the unknown always trumps the known.

Mostly I feel relief. I am a convicted murderer, sentenced to life without the possibility of parole, and I am going to the joint. My life as a free person, such as it was, is over. I don't even think about the loss of freedom. I just wonder if the food is as good as the storytellers would have you believe.

The ride to Chino runs through a gradually receding level of urbanization. The bus is a long double axle, not unlike a school bus but for the barred windows and the armed deputies. Pulling out of the back yard of the jail, we bounce down the potholed streets of old Los Angeles. It's still dark, the morning an idea pushing into the hazy air. I sit against one of the windows, part of a four-man shackle favored by the jailers, my face inches away from the dirty Plexiglas etched with gang insignia.

The only signs of city life at this hour are the knots of men huddled in storefronts and the anxious customers crowded around the dozens of bail bond outfits. Churches are everywhere: small, dingy places with bad paint and crooked hand-lettered signs. Hookers, their shifts ending in the coming daylight, are leaning against beat-up cars, smoking long, slim cigarettes. Patrol cars are at every intersection, down every side street, bristling with radio antennae and force. This is the last time I will see urban America. The lights and action and energy flash by as the bus picks up speed, pulls onto the freeway, and steams away from the city. In the next hours, as the sun struggles through the smog of the Basin, we travel into the suburbs of the San Gabriel Valley, out to the dusty farmland of the Inland Empire. The placidity of dairy cows replaces the frazzled electricity of fallen men and women in the pressurized anonymity of the city. How I loved those damaged women, their desperate longing for connection, their neediness a delicious magnetic thing. The road through the free world and its excitements ends when we arrive at the Reception Center Central, surrounded by gun towers and barbed wire, smoldering in the omnipresent stink of cow shit.

All intake units in prison are alike—holding tanks, cardboard boxes with our property scattered around, and angry guards. After the ritual strip search, I am issued my first set of prison blues: a blue chambray shirt with metal buttons, a pair of blue jeans, underwear and socks, and a State of California identification card. I am assigned the prison number C-19449, which will henceforth be more significant than my name; it is the number under which all my records will be stored. All the misdeeds of my life, my entire identity, are wrapped up in those digits.

In the next six weeks I will be tested numerous times, interviewed by a psychiatrist for fifteen minutes—he will diagnose me as suffering from an antisocial personality and an aggressive reaction to adolescence—and appear before my first committee. I only realize years later that the prison system functions as a mega-committee, and the lower-level committees are like the individual cells of its body. A great prison writer of the past, Eddie Bunker, described prison as "no beast so fierce." With all due respect to an elder, I would describe it as no committee too trivial.

The Guidance Center, built in the 1930s, is a long corridor out of which spring eight wings of three tiers each. Named after trees, they are each designated for different types of prisoners. I end up in Cypress, Two West, along with the other violent offenders, murderers and robbers, most of them young and rebellious. The fronts of the cells, in the form of closely spaced bars, face the outer shell, fenestrated by long, tall windows broken out by years of collective unhappiness. Every night the fires begin, mattresses and blankets thrown out across the space between the tiers and the walls of the building. They catch in the broken mechanisms that once opened and closed the missing windows and flare up, lighting the darkened building with fleeting shadows and cascades of sparks. Along the floor of the bottom tier are smoldering piles of partially burnt debris mixed with shards of glass, a smoking mass that is swept out of the block every morning.

All day and night an incessant chatter fills the wing: war stories of imagined past glories, convictions endlessly dissected and reargued to a more favorable outcome, plans for successful futures after prison. It's the babble of those who can't come to terms with their new life inside, who are forced to reside in imaginary other lives. Scattered through this rabble of misfits are a few guys who stand out, less agitated, more comfortable in their own skins. We are drawn to one another, and seem to always end up in the same spots on the Reception Center yard.

One day I'm standing in a corner of the yard when Lizard approaches me. "Walk with me," he says. This is the invitation to serious conversation in the joint, and his demeanor demands my instant attention. In prison, there are classes of men, like everywhere else. His pants are pressed, his hair combed straight back and neatly trimmed, the mustache long at the ends, tattoos down each muscled arm. He speaks softly but with an intensity that carries force. But the most defining characteristic, the one I would come to know and recognize over and over again in these places, is a depth and flatness—he could have watched anything and nothing would penetrate the armor that scales his eyes. Though I'm still a teenager, I know he sees the same incipient hardness in my own eyes. He asks me: "Where are you from?"

Your hometown is a marker of your place. I hailed from Northtown, the ugly expanse of violence and failure sitting at the top of Long Beach. In those days, I was part of a large "car" of hardheads who had walked Artesia Boulevard and South Street before the bus delivered us to the netherworld of prison. In the coming ten years, my neighborhood would transition from poor and working-class whites to poor and working-class blacks; another decade and it would become a Mexican area. I was among the last of the whites who migrated to the joint. My older homeboys were infamous throughout the system. At some prisons, being from Northtown was cause enough for placement in the hole as a precautionary measure.

My neighborhood had earned its reputation for producing violent men long before I arrived. White low riders, or street thugs, surrounded on three sides by poor, minority cities and next to the solidly middle-class Lakewood, struggled against all. Race riots in the schools were an annual event, and the police rarely ventured in without extra cars. Fighting was a part of the normal course of things. I don't remember a time when there wasn't some feud going on between this little group or that one, always settled at drunken parties held in the boarded-up houses that lined the streets. Drugs were everywhere, and everyone used them. A boy who didn't do drugs was assumed to be a faggot or a snitch.

I had spent most of my teen years in and out of a variety of juvenile facilities for one infraction or another. The truth was, I felt safer behind bars than out in the streets; freedom was more terrifying than confinement. The last time I'd been allowed out from the Paso Robles Youth Authority in December of '79, I had moved back in with my family—the first of a series of bad decisions. I moved out a week later, after a bitter argument that ended with my tearing the door off its hinges, my worldly belongings tossed, once again, into a green trash bag. My immediate descent into the world of drugs and nihilistic self-destruction had put me at odds with my parents' world of barely repressed rage and regret. We all breathed a sigh of relief as I pulled away in my '65 Chevy van.

I wondered afterward why I hadn't done it earlier. Before I got out from my last stint, I was offered jobs and placement hundreds of miles north of my family and my neighborhood. My parents practically demanded I move back in with them, and for reasons I'm only now beginning to understand, I did.

It was a disaster from the start. My younger brother and sister hadn't even been consulted. For a welcome home dinner, there were fish sticks. I piled my food into the middle of the plate and started shoveling it in until I noticed no one was talking. They were all staring at me using only my spoon and hunched over, defending my food. Later, I wore my boxers and socks into the shower to wash them by hand. After enough time, jail becomes your norm and you carry it around with you wherever you go. That's why ex-cons can spot each other in a crowded room; they hear the clang of bars and smell the wariness that separates those who survive from those who don't.

There was no honeymoon period. The fights and accusations started the next day, as if I had only been gone for the weekend. The underlying tension of my parents' union continued to be the great, unspoken dynamic of our family. They hadn't shared a bed since I was a young boy, and none of us could recall any outward display of affection, not a kiss or a hug. The anger in our house, the force that held the drapes shut and pushed me out into the streets, originated in the failure of my parents' relationship.

My mother had been a wild young woman. Pregnant and married at seventeen to her first husband, nicknamed "Tiger," she was possessed by the terrible tragedy of her youth. Abandoned by her father, and then orphaned by her mother's death in the Cocoanut Grove fire in Boston, she lived in a state of torment. She raged at the vicissitudes of cruel fate, particularly at the day she got pregnant with me—which, she regularly observed, was the worst day of her life.

Her union with my father seemed doomed from the start. He had been orphaned at a young age in the Great Depression, and had a failed marriage behind him as well. Ten years her senior, he was emotionally already dead. Nevertheless, or perhaps on account of their unhealed wounds, they remained locked together until death parted them.

My mother spent a considerable amount of energy pointing out all of my father's inadequacies. There she would be, five feet and ten inches of black-haired, green-eyed fury, shouting how he had ruined her life; she could have married a rich man. This had been going on for all of my conscious life. I used to wonder how it was that he hadn't killed her.

And there were money problems, always money problems. My father worked his ass off trying to sell life insurance, but he was a retired enlisted man with no formal education. It's not that he lacked intelligence; he lacked the ability to connect in a friendly way. All the years of suffering had burned that out of him.

The first time their unhappiness drove me out of the house, I ended up being arrested for running away; it was my father who turned me in. Their misery invaded my body and made me ill. Around the age of twelve I began to experience terrible pain in the gut, so severe it would double me up on the ground as if I was being kicked by some unseen presence. Many trips to the Navy hospital and multiple grueling tests later, it was clear nothing was physically wrong with me. Eating hostility and anger for breakfast, lunch, and dinner had torn my insides up.

A couple of weeks after I ran away, the police showed up where I was reinventing myself as a stagehand for the Long Beach Civic Light Opera—taking advantage of the free dinner and the chance to meet liberated, artsy women—and made a big show of arresting me, slapping on handcuffs and roughly shoving me out to their car. As I was being pushed into the back seat, I saw my father across the street, leaning against the fender of his Delta 88 Oldsmobile, his tired face lit in orange-and-black chiaroscuro each time he took a drag on his Lucky Strike. I knew right then this was a charade put on at his request.

The cops drove me the seven miles downtown in dead silence. I was hustled in to booking and subjected to a lot of yelling and harsh treatment—the cops seemed to enjoy the freedom to be tough on an arrestee. After sitting in a holding cell for hours, I was brought to another small tank. Perched in the back was an older guy, probably in his thirties, handcuffed and waist-chained. Obviously the stage had been set for a good talking to by someone who had been there, done that. He started asking me questions, prodding me to rethink my ways, to return to the straight and narrow. At one point, he appeared to have a revelatory moment and grew quiet. He had been putting on quite a performance. I'm sure his intentions were sincere: no one wants to see a kid headed to our world. Finally he offered me a cigarette and spoke to me in a completely different tone, one of coconspirator. "You're either going to get killed soon or die in prison," he said. We both laughed and blew smoke rings in the stale shadows of Long Beach City Jail.

When my father came to pick me up, he had the self-satisfied air of someone who believes he's made a difference. I was so furious with him I couldn't speak. He told me he hoped I had learned a lesson. I had, but not what he expected. I had discovered the joy of being arrested, when the entire world comes to a stop and focuses on you, a heady thing for a boy who felt torn apart by primal forces at home and didn't easily fit in anywhere else. Sitting in that small cell, I had met a comrade, a fellow traveler on the road to oblivion. He had felt it too, I'm certain, this deep connection. I also learned not to trust my father. Whatever tenuous links had held us together were severed forever. Although he made a few half-hearted attempts over the coming years, it was over between us. To this day, he often seems like some sad man who was around when I was little, and hardly ever as I grew up. I never learned who he really was.

*

At Chino, whenever our group goes to the yard, I carry a well-crafted shank that fits snugly in my shoe. Only six months before, on that same yard, a black-white battle had left one man dead and many seriously injured. The preparation for war is always ongoing. All around me, other young men are being groomed by the older members of their groups. The armies of the dispossessed and disenfranchised are poised to wage futile, pointless wars over patches of dead grass and dirty concrete owned by the government. In the juvenile jails and prisons, even in the county jail, the struggle tended to be disorganized and moved by no ideology. It was primitive. In prison, it's different. There is tremendous organization and direction, illusory as it is.

It's at Chino that I first encounter the degree to which prisoners control the life of a prison. This is another new experience for me. At every level, in every corner and facet of the joint, prisoners influence what happens. The day I'm processed into prison, I notice that prison guards do little of the actual work; they mostly supervise. A prisoner-clerk types all my personal information onto a flexible card. The photographs are taken by a prisoner who arranges the numbers over my name on the mug board and captures for all time the extent of my removal from society. Fingerprints, bed roll, and cell assignments are all done by men in blue chambray shirts and jeans. I would later refer to them as "citizens," these men who provide the grease for the machine to grind forward.

I spend six weeks at Chino, in the Guidance Center, stewing in the acrid, manure-laced air, walking around the track with Lizard and waiting for my ride up north. I'm slated for transfer to San Quentin. To this day, there is a mythical note to the term "up north." The latest end-of-the-line prison, Pelican Bay, at the very northernmost tip of California, adds even more weight to the phrase.

Back when I came to prison there were only four serious joints: Soledad, Tracy, San Quentin, and Folsom, with a bunch of lesser places for the less serious. The big four were all far north of Los Angeles. Soledad—"The Dad"—had been the scene of some of the major events in California prisons in the '60s and '70s. Tracy was usually called "Gladiator

School" because younger guys went there, and that's just what it's like when young, angry guys are crammed together. San Quentin—"S.Q."—in the San Francisco Bay area, home to death row, was known for its wide-open, Wild West character. Folsom—"The Pit"—was the end of the line with its huge granite walls, massive gates, rifles bristling out of every conceivable crevice; it was so menacing that it seemed unreal, a television fantasy of a prison.

Being transferred to San Quentin is a major opportunity. It means that I'll have a chance to be invited into the upper caste of prisoners, those who actually run the prisons and live a different life from the masses. The pass into this realm is a series of tests that grow increasingly difficult: holding knives without panicking, standing guard while someone is beaten or stabbed, running drug dealing businesses—all of these leading to an invitation into the circle of leadership.

On the day of my departure, I carry a few messages, letters of introduction, guys there in my property.

I end up at The Dad instead.

Soledad-Central

No one ever explains to me the reason for the crossed wires. Apparently, no one sufficiently explains it to the prison either. At my first committee, one of the members asks me what I'm doing there, given that I have a sentence of life without the possibility of parole. Soledad doesn't have lifers. I respond that the bus driver told me to get off; it wasn't my call. This doesn't go over well. I'm advised that I can go to their yard, but the transfer paperwork to San Quentin will be processed immediately.

Before the authorities at Soledad manage to file their request, my crime partner, Bob, is sent to San Quentin. As they don't like to put codefendants on the same yard, the prison's request is denied, and I'm put up for transfer to Folsom. This, too, is denied because I don't meet the minimum age requirement. Now Soledad files a request to override the age issue because of my extreme dangerousness and criminal sophistication at the age of nineteen. As it turns out, by the time this battle between committees is resolved and I'm ordered to be transferred to Folsom, I'm already in the hole for a battery.

The jobs for thugs in prison are limited. I become an enforcer for a drug dealer. Frank is in his mid-thirties, has done a solid decade or more, and deals drugs for profit. He spots me a couple of weeks after I arrive. I am penniless, aimless, and filled with an endless supply of rage. My days are spent on the iron pile, slamming around until I can barely lift my arms. At night I am trapped in my cell watching the paint peel, a practice that is more colorfully called "wallavision." Frank asks me if I want to make some money, and sets me up in his business.

I sell bags of pot for canteen and mail-outs. I smoke my cut. Collection is a matter of waiting for bags of instant soup and coffee and smokes. Frank lets me know when the money lands at his place in the "free world" from a mail-out. The system works like this: I sell you a hundred bags and give you a free-world address where the money needs to be sent.

You have ten days. After ten days it doubles, and every ten days thereafter it keeps doubling. There are no acceptable excuses for why it's late. It's a harsh but efficient system. For this to work there have to be penalties for those who fail to make adequate and timely payments.

Kenny Wilson doesn't pay on time. Worse, he objects to the late fee and complains, even stating he won't pay the tax. He becomes my first big test. After he makes his stand, I run into his cell and hit him in the gut so hard he starts vomiting. I reiterate the rules and tell him all the money better be there by the end of the second ten-day period. Later that night the goon squad appears at my door and escorts me to administrative segregation, informing me I'll be talking with the captain the next day. As is common in prison, no reason is given. As the U.S. Supreme Court wrote in one of its more ghastly opinions, a trip to the hole is an expected part of serving time, for any reason or no reason at all.

The next morning, I'm brought into an office, in handcuffs, where Kenny sits, not in handcuffs, and the captain. He explains that Kenny can't afford to pay the interest, but the principal will be paid at the next canteen draw. I feel triumphant at this moment. Here I am in prison, one of the legendary joints in the largest prison system in the country, a new recruit, and I am being treated as a predator. I am, in fact, a predator. I act on the ethos that if you can't defend what I want, I am entitled to it. Being accorded this perverse deference, I feel like a free agent, massive and justified, beholden to no one and nothing. I agree to accept the lesser payment in exchange for placement back into the general population. Before dinner, I'm back in my cell.

I know right then that Soledad isn't for me. I need a bigger challenge, more pain and violence, more suffering. Walking into the chow hall that night, I observe the world I live in more closely. Up in one corner in a cage about twenty feet off the floor sits a fat guard armed with a shotgun. He looks out over a room of about twenty square yards, down the center of which we walk to the steam tables. If you turn right, you go down the line to the Northern Mexican and black side; left takes you to the Southern Mexican and white side. The walls have pock marks in them from forty years of buckshot sprayed at the first sign of trouble. The tables are stainless steel octagons with four seats welded at the base. Each subgroup within the stark divide has its own group of tables. Brushed aluminum salt-and-pepper shakers are on each table, along with black plastic ashtrays. Everyone in prison smokes these days. The food comes out of huge pans, ladled onto the stainless steel tray you hold in front of you. It is standard institutional fare—lots of butter, bread, and grease, with some meat thrown in if you are lucky. During my brief stay at Soledad, I never see the chow hall erupt in open warfare, but the tension is always there on the faces of the prisoners and the guards. Large groups of angry men in chow halls are the scourge of the prison system.

The same divisions are found on the iron pile. Soledad's yard is, by the standards of these places, huge. Two times around the track equals a mile; at most prisons that number is closer to four or five. At each corner stands a tower with an armed guard. The weight pile, filled with tons of pig iron and crudely fashioned machines, runs almost the length of one side of the rough square of the yard. Each group works out only with its own, using its own benches and rarely speaking to the others. I continue my ferocious workout pace, growing bigger by the day. Someone is stabbed on the yard about once a week, but it has little impact on my life. As long as the stabbing doesn't cross racial lines, the administration doesn't seem to care.

At least not until a guard is stabbed by a deranged guy fresh out of the hole. The entire place is locked down, and the retaliation begins. Every cell is searched, or rather trashed, in an orgy of violence that looks and feels an awful lot like one gang responding to another gang's trespass. This goes on for weeks, during which time there are no showers, no canteen, no yard, no nothing outside of the cell. I would learn this is the form of punishment used most often in California prisons—long periods of cell time and punitive searches. That it never works to deter negative behavior is beside the point.

After a few weeks of being locked in a cell without any outside time, a man undergoes definite personality changes. By the time the cages are reopened, everyone is more wary than usual, as the personal space of each prisoner is expanded. I also learn a few things about myself during that first extended lockdown. I don't mind being restricted to the eight-by-ten confines of my cell. I work out daily. I don't have to interact with anyone but my cellmate. Later, I realize that the effects of the separation from others during a lockdown are a cumulative experience; it stacks up inside. Most important, I learn that the level of my internal anger is overwhelming. A couple of days after we're released from lockdown, I run into Kenny's cell and beat him unconscious.

I take all his property out of his cell and give it to anyone passing by; no one turns down the offer. The guards find him during count time. Before the end of the evening, I'm in handcuffs, on my way back to the hole.

Just as there are a few famous pens, there are a few famous holes in California's concrete-and-iron empire. The O wing, the Security Housing Unit at Soledad, is among the better known. As I'm being processed into this prison within a prison, the first thing I see is a blown-up X-ray print of what is obviously a shank inside a human colon. The message is clear: do not hide shanks in your ass because they can pierce you from the inside out, leading to peritonitis and usually death. I have never keistered anything more menacing than a balloon full of dope; I'm impressed by the level of commitment, if not by the results. I'm assigned to Two West, looking out over four small exercise yards, one for each group, and the blank wall of another building. The cell has closely spaced bars, further demarcated by a tight metal mesh. Every weld and point of pressure is spray-painted fluorescent orange. There is a simple bed, bolted to the wall, and a locker hung up on the back. A toilet-and-sink combo completes the furnishings. I'm issued a twelve-inch black-and-white television with the speaker cut and a simple earplug. Food is brought to the cell three times a day, Yard is twice a week for a couple of hours, and showers are three times a week. I never leave the cell until I'm strip-searched and placed in handcuffs with two guards escorting me.

Shortly after I go to the hole, I am notified that my transfer to Folsom had been approved a couple of days before I decided to beat Kenny down. Because of the rules infraction incurred, I have to stay at Soledad for the time being. I'm found guilty of battery and given a nine-month hole term. The wheels are set in motion for transfer to The Pit. I while away the time in the hole, staying up late watching old movies, exercising, and conjuring up images of Folsom.

Thus far, prison has been a letdown. I had expected to come up against seriously hard men, to see things no one should see. Soledad has been soft, and I have run amok in the months before the hole. Most of the prisoners I meet are more concerned with staying out of trouble and getting out, and getting high in the meantime. There is always talk of going home, but I don't feel like I have a home to go to.

*

I'm in waist chains and leg irons, being escorted out of O Wing by several guards. The entire bus is filled with the troublemakers, the rowdy assholes of Soledad heading for Folsom. This is the beginning of a great shift, one of the periodic great shifts in the California prison system, sending all of the worst, most incorrigible, angriest prisoners to Folsom. I'm about to board the first bus out of Soledad. As I walk out into the dusky light of the early morning, the captain who had negotiated Kenny's payment plan stands directly in front of me. He tells me I'm going to where I belong. I tell him, "Fuck you and your punk-ass prison." I'm hustled onto the bus and secured in one of the tiny high-security cages at the front. There is energy on this bus I key into immediately. We are all on a great adventure, headed to the most feared and respected joint in California. I'm excited, and probably a little scared, like right before a

roller coaster ride starts, or right before a punch connects
with your jaw.

Folsom State Prison: I

The ride to Folsom takes us up the Central Valley, through
dry, rolling hills and miles of farmland, small towns hugging
the interstate. We pass through the outskirts of Sacramento,
the state capital, and into the little city of Folsom, grown
around the citadel of suffering. We get our first look at the
prison late in the afternoon, when long shadows throw the
piles of granite into high detail. It is gray—a dull, lifeless gray
that sucks all the energy out of the bus. On several return
trips to this prison, I notice the same effect. An oppressive
sense of doom radiates outward from the blocks of stone. It's
on account of Folsom Dam that the address to the prison is
Represa, Spanish for dam, but we prisoners always related
it more to the English word *repression*. Perhaps *dam* is even
more accurate, as Folsom State Prison was built to hold back
and contain—and serves no other legitimate purpose.

The bus pulls into the sally port, an underground passage,
between the Romanesque vault of the West Gate. Gun posts
are at every corner, manned by men in mirrored sunglasses.
Across the road stretches One Building, which holds 1,200
men in a single vast capsule, a giant concrete structure with
an oddly multicolored roof. The gatehouse leading into the
center of the building has an arch tall and wide enough to
drive a semi-truck through, with huge bars as thick as a man's

leg and steel doors out of some nightmare hallucination of a cathedral. The chapel made famous by Johnny Cash squats off to one side, another square structure in granite. The outside walls of Five Building, the original Folsom, run alongside the entryway, pockmarked by rifle shots.

The bus stops under 14 Tower and we are directed out, assembled in a ragged line under one of the ubiquitous rifle barrels about twenty feet above our heads. There is no sound, not even muffled coughing; the walls have swallowed all of that. An old, red-faced lieutenant greets us. Here comes the ritual pep talk, I think to myself. We'll be told to behave, that our good conduct will be rewarded, that they strive to create and maintain a safe and peaceful environment—all the usual nonsense. Instead, after stubbing out his cigarette and coughing out a wad of phlegm, he gives us two statements of fact and two admonitions: "This is Folsom Prison, and the rules of the rest of the goddamned CDC don't mean shit here. If you try to escape, we'll kill you. If you put your hands on one of my guards, we'll kill you. Other than that, we don't give a shit what you do to each other." At that, he turns around and walks away. No more accurate description of Folsom is ever offered. This is prison at it its most elemental.

Along with the rest of the bus, I'm escorted to the hole to complete my term for the battery of Kenny. Because of the influx of rowdies, the entire back section of One Building, comprising three hundred cells, has been turned into Security Housing Unit II. The cells at Folsom are about five by seven feet, smaller than a closet or a half bath, with open bars. Inside the superstructure of the building are five tiers, with sixty cells across the front and sixty cells across the back of each. Along the inside of the outer shell run two narrow walkways, each manned by a gunner armed with a semiautomatic rifle and a .38-caliber sidearm, in case one of us is mad enough to jump across the chasm onto the gun walk. At first I'm assigned to a single cell because I have life without the possibility of parole, but that will change when more bodies are crammed into Folsom than it was designed to hold.

A day or so later, a guard comes to my cell and asks me which yard I want to go out to. I ask what the options are. He says I can ask for P.C. or go to the fellas' yard. I'm not about to ask for protective custody, so he approvingly escorts me to the other yard.

One of the first things I notice about Folsom is how they move maximum-security prisoners around—without handcuffs and with only one guard. Their philosophy on this is pure Folsom. They don't put us in handcuffs because every man has a right to defend himself if attacked, which occurs daily, and they aren't going to defend us, ever. There is only one guard because each guard is assumed to be able to handle himself; if he can't, he shouldn't be working there. This Folsom attitude goes right up to the wardens, who all walk the yard, by themselves, embodying the spirit of violence and force that pervades the prison. It all makes perfect sense to me.

*

It's about four in the afternoon, and I'm standing in front of One Building. Because the new unit has only recently opened, there are no little caged-in areas like at Soledad. We're restricted to an area about the size of a basketball court. This is the fellas' yard, "the fellas" being the universal nickname for the fabled white prison gang that dominates Folsom. I'm twenty years old, and I have rocketed to the very pinnacle of California's prison world. The men on this yard are legendary. They all have nicknames and miles of ink tattooed across their bodies. There is a palpable sense of barely suppressed rage in the way they walk and interact. They're like cowboys of the gunslinger type; they command a certain degree of respect, even when clad only in their boxer shorts, as we all are. I want to be one of them so badly it hurts. I want to be referred to as "brother" by a fellow prisoner. I want to redeem my shame and guilt at being in prison, at having fucked up my entire life, by achieving the dignity they wear with such nonchalance. I've never been so impressed in my life.

On a yard like this little compressed one, populated by true hard cases, it's rare for anyone to come up and talk to you. People have to be weighed and sized up—friend or foe, acceptable or not acceptable—and prisoners learn the fine art of character assessment as a part of learning to survive. I stand there in the shadow of all that concrete and granite, in the hole of the worst prison in the land. Out of a corner of the building, a small, bald-headed old man, wearing a pair of purple briefs, walks up to me. I'm dumbstruck by this radical incongruity. He reaches out, snatches the front waistband of my boxers, and peers in. "What you working with, youngster?" he asks. I have no idea how to respond. The cowboys are laughing. One of them shouts out, "Leave the boy alone, Millie." The ice is broken. I'm invited to play basketball.

My first committee meeting starts off with the chairman telling me I'm too young to be at Folsom, and that they won't be releasing me out of the hole even though my term is up. I don't crack wise: the atmosphere of the place tends to dry up that kind of response before it leaves your mouth. Instead I file an appeal and spend the next two months fighting to be released to the main line of The Pit. One day, with no warning, the sergeant comes to my cell and tells me I'm being released, right now. On the way to the front of the building, he predicts I'll be dead or will kill someone by the end of the year.

The sergeant walks me to the gate. He tells me to go across the yard and see Tony, the convict behind one of the windows in the low-slung administration building: "Tell him you just got out of the hole and need a cell." I head out into The Pit. There is no mob screaming "New meat!" or any of that Hollywood crap—that never happens. The powers that be already know who I am, what yard I was on, and to what position of the social structure I will be assigned initially. I walk up to the grated window and tell Tony my story. He knows I'm serving life without the possibility of parole and offers me a single cell—second tier, A section, One Building. I am now a resident of Folsom, this granite circle of Hell.

James Posten, a great prisoner-writer, described Folsom State Prison in the early '80s as a "riot in slow motion." Arriving with the first wave of the new worst of the worst, I'm the second-youngest convict on the yard. The old men who have seemingly grown out of the granite are still there, though their time is fast ending. Folsom, unlike any institution I've ever been in or ever will be again, has a strict routine. Breakfast, lunch, and dinner are the same time every day. Yard release, yard recall at the sound of the archaic steam whistle, workers streaming into and out of the tag plant, education classes, and religious services all happen at their appointed hour. But a reminder of the constant potential for instability sits atop a wall by the front gate: the .30-caliber Browning Automatic Rifle, installed after Machine Gun Kelly stormed the wall, killed the warden, and escaped into the countryside way back in the Great Depression. Once a month, the machine gun is tested against the far wall of the riverbank, across from the prison. The sound cuts through your soul, a wrenching reminder of the primacy of force.

I'm the newest embodiment of this latent anarchy— I'm young, angry, devoid of direction, and I don't fear any established order. Over the next couple of years my peers pour in, exiled from the rest of the prison system, sent to where they, too, belong. The thinking is that we will be intimidated into compliance by the rigors of The Pit. What ultimately happens is that we upend the place in an orgy of bloodshed and chaos.

In those couple of years, Folsom is transformed from the rigid, orderly world I found there into a dystopian nightmare. The various gangs, flush with a surplus of willing soldiers, launch campaigns against one another, and against their respective members, with a ferocity the place has never seen before. This is unlike previous spikes in violence; no one charges the walls to test the resolve of the guards. Rather, we turn on each other. Before the prison system breaks it up and transfers the worst of us out to the new maximum-security joints, hundreds will be stabbed. Dozens will be killed.

My first year, I do what any other self-respecting thug would do: lift weights and deal and do drugs. Each of the three groups—blacks, whites, and Mexicans—actively recruits soldiers to their standing armies. The leaders, no doubt astonished that the prison system has decided to send them an endless supply, work their respective forces to combat readiness. Since the last of the big black-white battles of the late '70s, there has been an uneasy truce between these two groups. The yard, no bigger than a small town square, has areas each claims as its own. The basketball court in front of One Building and the areas around the boxing ring belong to the blacks; the trashcans over by the canteen are held by the white leadership; the handball courts next to them by the Mexicans. The commons are in between these two areas. There's a baseball field ringed by a six-foot-high chain-link fence. A movie that filmed just before I arrived (*The Jericho Mile*) resulted in the construction of a track—twelve times around equals a mile. Bleachers sit off to one side of the field. At one end of the yard is the canteen with its long rails like a ride at Disneyland. At the other end is the Yard Shack, an octagonal building that holds the basketballs, handballs, horseshoes, and the occasional shank in one half, and the yard guards' office in the other.

Off to one side, way in the back through a creaky turnstile, is the iron pile. Like everywhere else, it's divided into tribal regions. Within the whites' area are about ten benches surrounded by all the necessities of weightlifting—straight bars, curled bars, plates called quarters, dimes, and nickels, dumbbells ranging in size from 20 pounds to 110 pounds apiece. The best bench on this part of the pile, with the more advanced Olympic iron and festooned with green shamrocks, belongs to the fellas. The system works in shifts; the morning shift is for the more serious. One of my older homeboys offers me a spot on his morning team. Butch runs the team like a drill sergeant, with more rules than one can easily remember. The bottom line is: *be on time.* Tardiness is inexcusable and results in banishment to a lesser team. I am never late.

It's early one winter morning, and the rain is pouring down, splish-splashing on the stone. I've been at Folsom for several months now. I've carried around knives, held great caches of weapons in my cell, delivered bags and bags of dope; I've passed all the requisite pre-tests of prison character. I make my way out through the One Building gatehouse, known as the "count gate." I am easily twenty pounds heavier than when I arrived, with nineteen-inch arms and a bulging chest. I have adopted the Folsom attitude required of all up-and-coming young white thugs. I will brook no trespass of my personal space. I am a warrior in a violent cult of the dispossessed. But there are still rules.

I notice the yard is mostly empty. I make my way to the bench to set everything up. It's chest day, so I stack the quarters deep on either side of the head of the bench, grab the bigger dumbbells, and smooth out the wet blanket. I drink deeply of my tumbler of coffee. (Butch is constantly trying to get me to drink his honey-and-coffee concoction—he swears by it. I think it tastes like shit. I want my coffee so bitter it leaves its trace on my tongue like battery acid.)

I take a deep pull on a cupped Camel; can't smoke during the workout, no puff and buff. The rain keeps pouring down, but it doesn't clean anything, just makes it all wet. On the hill up above the pile, I can see the concrete legs of the giant gun tower that dominates the scene. There's no counting how many have died in here over the years. The granite that looms all around bears the same scars we do. At the back of the pile, the rock face rises a good thirty feet, the marks of the quarrymen who pulled free the blocks for the wall and the buildings clearly visible a hundred years later. At the bottom of this rock face is a long, narrow pool of water, fed by the weight of the hill above, weeping into the crevice. Swimming in the pool are all manner of fish, their wild colors and flowery fins weirdly out of place in this gray, gray world. (At Folsom, in those days before it all came unhinged, fish tanks were all the rage. The pool served as a breeding pond.) I wait and wait. No one shows up. The next morning I tell Butch of my dedication. He congratulates me on my adherence to the rules. I feel the way any boy does when his father praises him.

Daily life has a routine quality. Get up before the bars are racked because you never want to be caught sleeping with the door to the cell open. The bottom-bunk guy fires up the hot pot for the morning coffee. Generally, he makes the cups for both men and passes a lit cigarette up in an ashtray to the top-bunk guy. Some low-volume music. Not much talk. Waking up in prison is never a pleasant experience; cheery morning greetings seem a little mad inside of a prison cell. The guards come by to open the cell locks with their huge, medieval brass keys. The cells remain closed behind a long iron bar that is moved at the front of the tier by the guard for mass releases. When breakfast is called, the bar is pulled back and sixty men step out of thirty cells. We head down the stairs, down the flats of the first tier; the five tiers of the block, an immense presence, lean over us. Then in we go through the giant steel doors that are locked up each night to seal off the building.

The menu is posted on a giant mug board. Through the steam line, our stainless steel trays weighed down and our stainless steel cups filled with the blackest of black coffee, we walk to the tables. At Folsom there is no division between areas in the chow hall; if you don't want to eat with someone at the next open seat, you take the next open table, by yourself if you want. At either end of the chow hall, up about twenty feet, is a long gun walk with at least one gunner, more if things are looking particularly grim. On both sides of the chow hall, directly across from each gun walk, the walls are scarred with dozens of bullet holes. The food is generally better than the usual institutional fare, both in quality and quantity. Fried eggs, with dripping yolks and crispy bacon, or cinnamon rolls with delicious, syrupy icing smeared all across the top and sides. The same items as most everywhere else, but prepared with much greater care. The cooks are a proud group of convicts. After breakfast, it's back to the cells until yard release, with the exception that some of the citizens are released earlier to work assignments. In the cell, there is time for another tumbler of coffee, a smoke, the morning dump, waiting for the yard to run and the day's struggles to begin.

I smoke dope nearly every day. I snort crank when it comes my way. Folsom is awash with drugs, and I'm swimming along like almost everyone else: when I've got it, I get high. I'm not alone in this predilection. The canteen sells Visine to get the red out of our eyes, and mouthwash to clean our breath. Lots of incense burns in the building. Of course it's illegal, but the guards, some of whom are profiting handsomely from the trade, look the other way most of the time.

Yard release sends the horde who don't have jobs, don't go to school, or don't have some other marginally useful duty to perform, out to the scrum. I hit the weight pile, put in my two or three hours, and spend the rest of the day posted up—doing ward duty—in our areas. Some days, nothing of consequence occurs. I often fall asleep, stoned, in the bleachers until yard recall at the sound of the whistle. Weekdays, the yard is light; most of the guys are at work. On the weekends, it's packed with close to three thousand convicts. Fast-pitch softball teams come in from the streets to play our team. The bleachers are packed with rowdy spectators—the prison team has only home games. The boxing ring comes alive on the weekends, too. We have a boxing program and street fighters visit from time to time. The prison boxers tend to be furious starters but run out of wind quickly. Grudge matches make for better entertainment. Never interracial, they are almost always between friends who have had a falling out. Inevitably, they turn into wild, shit-talking battles in which both guys end up bloodied and spent.

Now and then a local band will come in and play some music; we always appreciate the female singers and turn out in the hundreds for them, regardless of their talent. This is the Folsom of the past fifty years. Mostly older convicts serving life terms, worn out by the battles of Tracy and Soledad, they appreciate continuity and regularity. The prison is a community, fractured, but a community nonetheless. But you can already see the changes coming. One day, before an outside softball team arrives to play, gunshots ring out. Somebody in the bleachers is killed, rolling off the side in a bloody mess, causing a bunch of fans to start jumping out of his leaking way. The gunners don't like quick movement.

I'm waiting outside the One Building count gate. It's movie time and I already know who's going to get hit during the flick. He is oblivious to the fact that his best buddy is going to do it. Drug debts to the fellas. His pal will enter the inner circle as he proves his loyalty by being so sadly disloyal. This is the way of things at Folsom. The world I live in has a savagery and a level of duplicity that rival those of any medieval court intrigue. At the front of the chow hall, a huge, battered screen has been pulled down. We are all settling down to our regular tables; food is being brought out from the kitchen in the back—hot brownies better than anything mom ever made, at least my mom, big stainless steel pitchers filled with ice-cold milk and steaming coffee. Sitting at one of the in-group tables, I am served like royalty. At the back of the chow hall, at the top of a small bleacher unit, is the projection booth.

When the lights go down, the joints are lit up and the sweet pungency of marijuana fills the huge room. After the second reel, as the credits start to run, the intended target has a well-crafted shiv run into his back. He crumples to the ground. He lies one table over from me, bleeding out. I make no move until the majority of the crowd has stood to exit. My table gets up, the conversation never misses a beat, we stroll out. Several minutes later, a team of guards runs by into the chow hall. They run back out toward the hospital with an inert body bouncing along on the gurney. Although fifty people saw the whole affair, no suspect is ever arrested. The assailant moves another notch up the chain of command. He stands on the yard the next morning, laughing, shooting the shit like it's any other day. I don't think he feels anything, one way or the other.

It's December 28, 1981. My birthday. And just like in Merle Haggard's great song "Mama Tried," I've turned twenty-one in prison doing life without parole. The fellas have planned a party for me, over in the heart of the trash cans. In this gray, gray world, the occasion of a birthday, particularly for someone so young, demands attention. This is the first birthday party with guests I've ever had. I have now been on the main line of The Pit for almost a year. During this time, I have befriended the bridge crew of our forlorn, earthbound vessel, and I have worked my way up the ranks to within a few rings of the inner circle. I have easily passed all the tests—a sad testament to how effectively the Youth Authority prepared me for prison. My few youthful tattoos have been augmented with great swaths of ink across my back and shoulders—swastikas, dragons, skulls, demonic imagery, all the motifs of the world I live in, all the symbology for the storm of darkness swirling within me. I am bigger, stronger, faster, and a lot meaner after this year of graduate-level time. I know how to make deadly serious weapons, and I know exactly where to run the shank in for maximum effect. I have studied under masters of these dark arts. I am considered one of the leaders of my generation of prisoners, we who will accede to power one day. A product of the organization's strict training, I exude a palpable force. The embrace of death and disorder, of chaos and inhumanity, imbues me with a sense of invulnerability. I have the Folsom polish.

I'm invited to sit on one of the trash cans. I do, dazzled at being so much the center of attention. First, we smoke some dope. The running joke amongst the fellas is how much I look like a younger version of one of them—he's always being asked, "Where were you in 1960, brother?" The jokes fly; it's the moment to achieve a deeper connection. Now, because I can drink legally, the liquor arrives. I am shit-faced in no time. To top off all this revelry, this party in the shade of an armed gun post, one of the real old-timers strolls up, guitar slung across his chest. He starts the familiar strains of "Mama Tried." We are all singing along, a raucous chorus of drunken thugs. It is on this day that I'm moved another ring closer to the inner circle. I know it, and I know the whole yard has watched the spectacle. I am treated differently, with more deference, more caution, from then on.

Some afternoons I pass through the metal detector and head over to the library. It sits on the edge of a steep downward slope aimed at the lower yard, just below the level of the big yard. Once you walk down the pathway, it's as if the yard vanishes. I go down to check out a pair of headphones and, usually, a Tchaikovsky record for the player. Ever since I first heard his work in a music appreciation class one summer when the school system was still trying to convince me to live up to my potential, it has touched me profoundly. The librarian is an impassive, fat man. By using an extension cord, I can sit outside at one of the tables. They're just like the tables you see out in front of Taco Bell, with a big, hard, plastic umbrella. I smoke a joint and drift away to the melancholy Russian music. *Pathetique* can leave me in tears as I feel the frozen world, the frozen emotions, the depth and weight of the sentiment. Perhaps it is something in the tragic nature of great Russian art.

*

The sentence of life without the possibility of parole had only been around a couple of years, and no one really thought it meant what it said. At another of the many committee hearings a prisoner attends, shortly after I was released from the hole at Folsom, one of the administrators looked me in the eye and told me, "No one serves life; everyone gets out." He said this without guile or artifice. He believed it. I don't think I'd thought it through with any seriousness. I was in prison, in The Prison, and my expectations for a long life had never been high. In the meantime, I was determined to persevere, for no good reason but to prove I could survive, a species of obstinacy, I suppose. Whenever I told my story—to other prisoners, to staff or lawyers— everyone seemed to acknowledge the unfairness of it. I didn't think it unfair. The truth is I had lived a rotten life, and I had left a trail of destruction behind me. It's not that I felt guilty or remorseful, not then, not yet. I felt like I had purchased my own ticket, punched the stub, and now had to endure the ride. Nevertheless, consequent to an obscure technicality revolving around the judge's imprecision during sentencing, I was returned to Los Angeles County Jail to attend a resentencing hearing.

Los Angeles County Jail: II

As I'm turning in my property, a prisoner-worker tells me one of the guys going down on the bus with me is an informer against the Mexican super-gang. They will be greatly indebted to me if I kill him before he gets to court. I tell him I'll see if I can do him on the way down to the county. It looks like a great opportunity to raise my standing in the community. Unlike every other county in the state, Los Angeles sends its own buses all the way to Folsom to reclaim its wayward citizens. The power of the smoggy metropolis extends far beyond its borders. I'm issued a set of khaki clothes, the uniform of Folsom's out-to-court prisoners. Set off by my polished, brown, state-issued boots, dark tan, bleached-by-prison-sun-blond hair, and hugely muscled frame, I fancy myself the very picture of convict royalty. Even the sheriffs, never known for their ability to offer respect, recognize that the handful of us who get on the bus at Folsom are not regular miscreants to be casually abused.

The guy I'm plotting to kill on the way down is a small-ish, skittish Mexican I outweigh by a good seventy-five pounds. Since crossing ethnic lines is always complicated, I recruit Alex, the one other white convict on the bus, into the plan. All I need him to do is fend off the other Mexicans when I move on the rat. Their expected response will be to defend one of their own; it's unlikely they'll know of his transgressions. It's the way of things in our world that when I tell Alex I'm going to kill a rat, he immediately agrees to lend a hand. It would be unthinkable to do otherwise. He requests of me a price for his support, though. Apparently, Alex had suffered a massive overdose of heroin and only recently awakened from a coma. The upshot: his memory was severely damaged. Like all of us, he knows he's made many enemies. The trouble is he can't remember them all. I'm pretty sure he assumes I'm one of his crossed former partners at first, but he warms to me in the heat of plotting. He asks that I give him a heads-up if I notice any hostile glances directed his way. It seems a fair trade to me. Alex and I together weigh close to five hundred pounds, and he'll serve as a perfect blocker for the task at hand.

The plan we formulate is simple and brutal. As soon as we decamp the bus and are herded into one of the windowless holding tanks of the county jail, I'll jump on the rat and strangle him to death. Alex will fight off any potential defenders long enough for me to finish the job, and then I'll join him, if needed. When we're busted I will assume full responsibility and cut him loose, as the saying goes. Anyone raised by the state understands this doctrine—if more than one person is arrested for the same crime, the one who's most guilty has a moral obligation to accept responsibility and free the others. In my own case, on the night I was arrested, I told Bob I would cut him loose, instructing him not to talk to the cops until he talked to a lawyer. He didn't heed my advice and gave a series of damning, only partially true, at least partly coerced statements to the detectives. Even so, at the trial I took the stand and tried to exonerate him. His failure to understand the code resulted in a life sentence for being in the area when I killed Mr. Fellowes.

The plan to kill the rat is interrupted when the bus pulls into a small, rural county jail for the night. I'm studying the design of the building as we pull in—it's the job of a prisoner to pay attention to his surroundings—and it looks like the proverbial cracker box to me. For the first time in my many years of incarceration, I think of escape. We're pushed into what looks like a drunk tank. I decide my mission can wait and begin to scout out how to break through the ceiling into the cold night air. Alex, who is serving only a few years, agrees to help me as a matter of course. The rest of the tank, besides the rat, is a group of petty thieves and other low-level types. I prepare to bust out. For the rest of the night I dig into the ceiling with bare hands and brute force, sweat pouring down my back. It's dawn when I finally make it to the underside of the roof, only to discover this cracker box has thick, welded steel skin. The letdown is enormous. I had envisioned myself commandeering a car and setting out on a vast crime spree, dying in a hail of bullets somewhere in California's Central Valley. My prison legacy would be secure. No one would ever forget Horse, the nickname I gave myself when I was thirteen years old and playing at being a tough guy. So limited is my thinking, that's all I care about—my place in prison. The free world, the "real world" as we still call it, has ceased to exist for me. Worn out by hours of hard labor and the rush of adrenaline, I collapse on the bunk and decide to deal with the rat later.

Another day of travel, and I'm standing in a crowded holding tank in the booking front of L.A. County Jail. Nothing has changed—the same ritual degradation, the same sense of grimly marching into the back of an old coal mine. There are no windows in the county jail. Once you're past the first series of tanks, the sky and sun become memories. I'm positioning myself to kill the rat. But at each step through the processing system, there's an impediment, mostly in the form of sheriffs. We're finally pushed into 4300, on the new side, about fifty guys crammed into a shower area designated for probably a dozen or less. One of the trustees is a friend from Soledad, an older Mexican named Black Willie, marginally connected to the big gang. Following the training of Folsom, I advise him of the situation and seek permission to do the job. With efficient calm, he gets me called out of the shower to meet with actual members. While I'm waiting, a much older Mexican comes up to me and says, "You would do this for us?" I assure him I will, I'm waiting on a piece. He leans in close, takes both of my hands, and tells me, "We won't forget you."

Black Willie comes and walks me over to an open cell, the light blinkered down, two hard-case Mexicans sitting at either end of the bottom bunk. One pats the bed in between them, and I sit down. Cigarettes are lit. I tell the tale, relate what I've been told. One of the Mexicans asks why I, a white guy, am willing to undertake this for them. It's to build my long-term relationship with their organization, I reply. I'm a mercenary. They seem extremely pleased, even impressed by my matter-of-fact attitude. Fellow travelers of the dark road recognizing one another in a dimly lit, concrete box. After satisfying themselves that I'm quite serious—and I am—one of them tells me this particular rat is no big deal, he's telling on his homeboys, not the clique. I can kill him if I want, but it won't be for them. I'm not in it for any high-minded principle, just personal advancement. I let it pass. His homeboys kill him a few months later.

Los Angeles County Jail: III

Back to the old side, back to the second floor and the high mods. The never-ending battle between the 5 percent of the population that is white and the 70 percent that is black has intensified. I'm assigned to 2600, delta row, cell 13, last cell on the tier. While standing in the dayroom waiting to go to my new home, I ask a young Mexican I've known over the years how many whites are in the module. He tells me the last one was carried out in a stretcher a few days ago. He looks concerned for me.

I get passed through the gates onto the tier, down to the very end. As soon as the bars to the cell close, I toss my shit on the bunk and start tearing out the light fixture at the back of the cell. (One of the fellas had clued me in on this source of knives before I left.) The three blacks in the cell are clearly stunned as I methodically take the frame apart with a nickel, pull it off, and pull out the metal plate.

I break off one side and stuff the rest back into the wall; best not to provide weapons stock to your enemies. As I start grinding the metal to a sharp edge on the floor, one of my cellmates breaks the pressurized silence: "What are you doing?" I tell him I'm making a knife, and that the first time I'm rushed someone is going to get the shit stabbed out of him. After a while longer, one of my cellmates asks me if I'm Horse from Northtown. I am. He says, "I know you. We were in the hole in the Y.A," He tells me he carries weight in this module: nothing will happen to me. I keep grinding away. I tell him that's all well and good, but I'll be packing everywhere I go. No one rushes me, no trouble; if they do, I'm prepared to put a lot of holes in them. I'm on my own, in the middle of a perpetual race war, and badly outnumbered. The only logical thing to do is brace for the worst. In the county jail the worst is always just around the next turn of the endless corridors.

The stalemate goes on for about a week. Everyone in the module knows I'm carrying a seven-inch, extremely sharp shank with me everywhere I go. Before each meal, the upper tier and the lower tier—a total of 130 restless, angry souls—are packed into a small dayroom to wait for the march to the chow hall. There's a large black-and-white television set up on the wall, secured inside of a steel mesh cage, but the televisions haven't worked since I was still standing around the neighborhood park dreaming up a cool nickname. I grab a corner, wedge myself into it, and stay alert. The tension is an invisible force that envelops the room. The hairs on my arms stand straight up. I'm determined to go out fighting.

A week into this crazy, untenable situation, I see Black Willie on my way to chow. He asks me where I'm living. After chow, a deputy announces on the loudspeaker to roll up my shit. I'm moving to 2100, the single-cell module down the corridor. As I walk down the tier, one of the young blacks yells out something about how I better be moving. I feel powerful, having held off the horde as long as I did, but I'm glad to be getting out. Black Willie is waiting for me when I walk through the front door of the new module. *They really don't forget*, I think to myself.

After the stymied war of 2600, 2100 is a kegger party. One of the deputies is running for a couple of the older whites, convicts both, and the drugs are flooding in by the cigarette pack full. (The way it works: The sister of one of the white convicts, a seriously hot, middle-aged featherwood—a tough little white girl, the female equivalent of "peckerwood"—named Donna, meets with the deputy and hands him a pack of Marlboros and $500. That same night he delivers the pack of smokes, which is packed full of heroin, coke, crank, and marijuana worth many thousands of dollars, inside the jail.) After I settle into my new private cell, I walk around to the upper tier to see Black Willie. I find him so sloughed he's barely coherent. He points to a loaded rig. Dark brown, liquefied tar heroin fills the barrel. "Go ahead, youngster," he tells me. I've never fixed dope before, but this is one of those moments when you step deeper in or pull back. I pick up the little rig, the needle ground down to a half-inch length, the barrel an inch-and-a-half hard plastic tube, the binky a small rubber piece of hose—a perfect prisoner-made kit.

I slip the needle into the crook of my arm, easily catching a vein. I can taste the needle's sharp, tangy, metallic essence as I wait for the telltale mushroom cloud of blood to push in through the viscous heroin. As soon as I register, I squeeze the entire contents in, not waiting or hesitating. I turn to hand the rig back, but Willie is in a deep nod, spittle trickling away from his mouth onto the little table with all his works. I throw a newspaper over the goods and head back to my cell.

I feel the taste of the heroin in the back of my throat. Its mixture of dirt and chemicals infuse every part of me. Collapsing on my bunk, I experience for the first time what happens when I shoot heroin: a tremendous warmth and sense of well-being combined with overwhelming nausea. Make yourself heave, everyone tells me. The trouble is I can't, no matter how hard I try. So I'm seriously stoned but immobilized on my bunk.

Although the race war has eased up in this module, it's not over. Skirmishes break out on a daily basis. Due to my Folsom demeanor and size, I'm thrust into being an unofficial representative for the few whites. The objective is to keep the business running, but circumstances ruin this plan. A big white guy from Chicago named Sarno gets in a beef with one of the ganged-up blacks. We negotiate for them both to take it to the dayroom, one-on-one, but the blacks had it planned out to rush in a group through the door. Before the wave of fellow gangbangers can run in, a big Mexican named Chuy slams the door to the dayroom shut, locking it. Sarno beats the black guy mercilessly. This doesn't go down well with the loser's homies. Another standoff, another round of negotiations, and the tension ratchets up another order of magnitude.

I grew up in an ethnically mixed neighborhood. I can't ever remember not being around blacks. I even knew a few well enough that we might have become friends if it hadn't been for the miles of ancient grudges that lay between us. Because of this, I tend to get along with most blacks. It's one of my black connections who comes to me shortly after the dayroom battle. He tells me the loser's homies are planning to stab me at the earliest opportunity. The next day, the deputies discover a weapons cache on the tier where these guys live. These two pieces of information compel me to act. I decide to lead an uprising of whites, all armed, and secure a segregated jail—being a member of a tiny minority can lead one to wild judgments. Using my influence with the Mexican group, I commission a group of their youngsters to manufacture knives. That night, an ominous scratching and grinding can be heard throughout the module. It's such a distinctive sound that anyone who has heard it instantly tightens up. Someone, or some group, is about to get stabbed.

The majority of the whites on the second floor are located in the module for those representing themselves in court without an attorney, known as "pro per" in legal jargon. I strap a dozen fresh shanks around my torso, hidden under my clothes and taped securely to my skin. Coming up with a plausible excuse to get into the pro per module, I approach the circle of white convicts. I'm a coil of raw, unfocused energy. This is one of those moments in my life when I'm reminded that I operate at a different level of viciousness.

I open my shirt and lay out the plan. We move together as a unit and inflict maximum damage. I'm on fire with zeal. My breath is labored from the surge of hate coursing through me, a thousand volts of pure rage. Before they say anything, I know this mission is beyond their capacity to shed reason. All of them claim some pressing need not to participate, revolving around court cases and release dates and bad omens.

Looking back on it now, I should have been more careful about building my case; instead, I nearly built my coffin. What happened the next day probably sealed my fate in prison.

I am holding the outer of the big grill gates open during chow release; my partner Silent is holding the other one open. When both are closed, they seal off an area of about ten feet square. In my left pocket is a seven-inch, double-edged, razor-sharpened shank. The handle is made from tightly braided strips of bed sheet material. I am alive in the moment, a death-dealing demon vibrating ever so slightly. My senses are functioning at a level I have never experienced before. I hear voices around me recede into the background, an indistinct hum. The two we are going to stab are last off the tier, as always. As soon as they pass through the inner gate I slam the outer gate shut; Silent slams his gate closed behind them. In one motion my shank tears out into the open and sinks to the hilt in the first victim's solar plexus, the force so great that for a brief instant he is balanced on the end of my arm, the knife a cruel fulcrum, our faces inches apart. I pull back from him and head for the second, passing the first to Silent. As this next victim realizes what is happening, as he feels the blast of my dark energy, he falls backward, away from me, away from the bloody shank dripping his friend's life force, and falls flat on his back on the floor. I pounce on him. He tries to cover his chest with his arms, rolling left to right. With my free hand I push his arms up and out of the way, ultimately sinking the piece into him about a dozen times before he goes limp. I leap up to see Silent in a desperate struggle with the first victim, whose longer arms are swinging furiously, keeping Silent mostly at bay. I grab the victim from behind by the hair, pull him toward me, and start running my shank into his chest and sides.

It is at this point, as the second victim is sliding to the ground, that the cacophony around me enters my consciousness. On the other side of the locked gates are dozens of enraged blacks, screaming in impotent rage, brought to a frenzy by the sight of two of their fellows massacred in a locked cage. Blood is everywhere. My left hand is dripping in a crimson flow. The deputies pop the inner door open from the central cage. The victim I left for dead on the floor comes up as if a string is attached to the top of his head. He runs down the tier, squirting blood. I turn to chase him down and somehow manage to accidentally sink the first couple of inches of the blade into the back of my own thigh. The other victim also vaults out of the cage, springing down the tier, clambering up an empty bunk bed onto the upper tier. The deputies are yelling, "Grab a hole! Grab a hole!" Silent and I both duck into the same cell as the bars rush together in a clanking shriek of metal on metal. A lone voice pierces the din: "See what you get, niggers."

A young Mexican kid is also in the cell. He grabs a towel and soaks it in the sink, washing the blood off my face and arms, turning next to Silent. The towel is leaking blood as if it, too, had been stabbed. Our host is so excited he can barely hold the two cigarettes he lights up for us; violence is both a contagion and a potent drug. I'm pretty much spent, smoking my Camel, still vibrating, as the deputies come pouring onto the tier. A senior deputy walks cell to cell. Stopping at the one Silent and I are in, he calls out the number. We are out on the tier, placed in handcuffs, and walked to the clothing room. All my clothes are confiscated as evidence. Barefoot, I'm placed in a jumpsuit and escorted out to the corridor, ordered to face the wall. The public address system starts blaring, "415, deputies involved," and my escort runs back into the module.

All the areas on the second floor with loose prisoners are in full revolt. Out of the back door of the module a line of deputies is pushed out by a mob of blacks; flashlights are flailing, the sound of a hundred steel-toed boots pound in the distance. Someone in the crowd yells, "There's that motherfucker!" About twenty feet separate me from the skirmish line, and the deputies are giving ground quickly. I turn to face the crowd and prepare to be rushed. One of the deputies realizes what's up and breaks ranks to run toward me. He puts an arm through mine and pulls me out of the corridor, down the escalator, and locks me into a small room. It takes hours for the floor to be restored to some semblance of order. Several deputies and dozens of prisoners are hurt. I am put in the hole. On the tier above I hear one of the victim's homeboys say, "That white boy,

Horse, he's a fucking assassin." I know, right then, I have achieved the vaunted status of a killer inside. A convict willing to take lives inside occupies an elevated place on the yard. The muscles of my left arm are ripped and torn from all the force I deployed. I hadn't just stabbed them; I had bashed them with the shank using all the power I could muster.

Neither of the two men I stab bed died, though not for lack of trying. I am charged with two counts of attempted murder and moved to the high-power module. I spend over a year fighting the charges, which are dismissed when the judge gets tired of seeing me in his courtroom; the victims are pressured by their homeboys not to testify; and the deputies who witnessed the attack have no interest in pursuing the case. To them, it is just another of the endless battles of Los Angeles County Jail.

*

It was this event that resulted in the beginning of my awakening as a human being.

It starts with a phone call to a lawyer's office and an overly curious girl. I'm a tier tender, and my friend Steve, whom everyone calls Popcorn, asks me to call his attorney and leave a message. I deliver it to the interesting voice on the other end. When she asks me what number Steve can be reached at, I tell her he's in jail and that he can't be reached. Then she asks me if I'm also in jail.

Yes

What is jail is like?

It's like one long day that runs for years and years.

The phone is at the front of the tier, right across from the front cell, Steve's cell. I deliver confirmation the message has been sent. The tier is twenty cells long, each cell a single with bars on the front. In this unit are the most dangerous, most famous, and most highly restricted prisoners of the county jail. Across from the front of the cells is a glass wall covered by reflective coating, a long, wavy, scary fun house mirror. They can see us, but we can't see them. Only one man at a time is allowed on the tier; on those rare occasions we end up together there is usually blood. Steve calls me back up to his cell.

Who was that on the phone?

I don't know, some chick at a law office.

You should call her back.

Why?

You two were hitting it off. Call her back. Here's a dime.

I dial the number, but a different voice answers. She puts Anita on the line. The silky and ingenuous quality of her voice draws me to her with an intensity I've never felt before.

Over the next year, I speak with Anita on the phone almost every day. After a couple of months, she says she wants to visit me. I'm seeing the occasional featherwood and lovely Donna now and then, but it's all part of the prison-world fantasy. I try to dissuade her, preferring to preserve the constructed image I have of her. She comes to visit anyway. She's wearing a burgundy raw silk outfit, with bronze-colored dangling earrings. She has luxuriant, thick, dark auburn hair down past her waist, and wide, green eyes in a golden brown Mexican face. Her beauty is nothing less than radiant. Always a talker, glib even, I'm stunned into a stammering silence.

All I know of Anita is her unhappiness, her sense of isolation trapped in a dysfunctional family of five brothers and a younger sister. Over many hours of conversation, I learn that she feels little connection to her parents and this resonates with my own story. The only difference is that she's middle-class and sees the world through that lens. My family, though not poor, was right on the edge; it's class resentment I feel. For some reason, still unclear, Anita is able to see something in me that I cannot see, something she cannot fully articulate. At the end of our visit, she tells me, "You are wonderful."

The words echo around inside my empty chest, hollowed out by years of keeping my distance from emotion—any emotion. For a moment, I feel as if I might cry. This is all too much. I'm securely shackled everywhere I go because I'm a menace, even in here. But a beautiful girl, an innocent, has managed to pierce me to the core of my isolation—past all the posturing, all the anger, all the fear and loneliness— with three words. She leaves. I'm escorted back to my cell in high-power, the most restricted section of the county jail.

Folsom State Prison: II

I'm on the Los Angeles County Sheriff's bus, heading back to Folsom. My place in this world is secure. I have made my bones, as the saying goes, and I'll be entering another, higher level within my group. Though only twenty-two, I'm a seasoned veteran of doing time the hard way. I know what it's like to be feared by everyone. In the whole county jail, there is only one place the deputies are referred to by their names alone—in high-power. Anywhere else it would be considered blatant disrespect and sufficient cause for an ass kicking. In high-power, the deputies know we'll fight back. A negative respect, to be sure, but it's intoxicating nonetheless.

I'm also considering this relationship, this irrational love affair that has entered my life. Over the next few months, Anita visits me almost every week. I begin to realize that she's never shared her secrets with anyone else. I become her confidant. In her imagination, I'm also a constructed figure, a perfect man devoid of flaws who loves her with a perfect devotion. She sends me beautiful pictures of herself in lingerie, and pages and pages of letters handwritten in her complicated, tortured script. She draws closer to me, pulled in by the force of my energy, dark though it is. I will come to know her in a way I've never known anyone in my life.

By no means am I a new man. I'm still the same thug that left Folsom thirteen months ago. If anything, I'm a lot harder, more determined than ever to burn a brief, vicious, white-hot flame. Still, somewhere inside the darkness, I detect within myself a scrap of humanity, buried and dormant. It's unsettling.

While I'm still sitting on fish row (new prisoners are referred to as fish), my friends plug me into a job in Receiving and Release, known as R&R in the joint. Whites have held the position since the granite cuts were still fresh on the blocks. Everything that enters or leaves the inner perimeter goes through R&R. People, goods, all of it must pass this century-old choke point. New arrivals are processed through, photos taken, property inventoried, and fish kits, which contain toiletries, envelopes, paper and a pencil, are issued. Parolees depart, leaving behind most of their possessions, although the occasional desperado can be seen lugging his shit out the gate, much to everyone's derision. Packages from family and friends come through R&R, a hole the size of a trash truck only recently plugged. We sell televisions and radios, we store weapons, and we engage in all manner of hustles, like all other prisoners. What sets us apart is the bridge to the real world, straight to the connection's house. We smuggle drugs. Mostly marijuana in pound increments. A few other things, now and then but primarily we hold the gate to the portal through which the bulky weed can flow. Everyone at Folsom smokes pot—including many of the guards. My first day on the job, John, a master smuggler and dealer who got me the spot, calls me upstairs on the pretense of a tour of the place. We sit up in the attic, a little nook behind the box storage area. He pulls out a brown wooden box, opens it, reveals a beautiful little pipe and starts loading a hit of brilliant green weed into the bowl. "You smoke pot, don't you?"

The first time I was asked that question was the first day of seventh grade, across the street from Hamilton Junior High School. For two years I had been in the Mentally Gifted Minor program, one class of thirty out of the Long Beach School District selected because of I.Q. test scores. My fourth grade teacher, Ms. Kimbrell, my first serious crush, had pushed for me to take the extra tests and my scores were, by all accounts, off the charts. I was sent to Madison Elementary School in lily-white Lakewood to start fifth grade with the sons and daughters of doctors and lawyers. Only two of us came out of Northtown, myself and Clifton Bowen, a big, goofy, good-natured kid with a mouth full of shiny braces. The experience was educationally positive, but it cemented my lifelong dislike of the rich.

After two years, I was slated to attend an accelerated high school program downtown. Neither my parents nor I were too enthusiastic about the daily journey, so I opted out and elected to attend the neighborhood junior high. That first day—new school, no friends—I recognized the local über-tough guy sitting across the street on his motorcycle. He belonged to the family that lived across the street from my family's house, one of a group of brothers, at least one of whom had been killed by the police in a botched jewelry store robbery some years past. Although we traveled in widely divergent circles, we were on friendly terms. He was generally acknowledged the baddest guy in the neighborhood—his fighting exploits were well known. He signaled me to come over with a slight nod of his head. I walked across the street. He pulled a joint out of his pocket, lit it with the mandatory Zippo, took a long hit, and passed it to me. "You smoke pot, don't you?" Of course I didn't, but my desperate desire to fit in, to be part of the accepted group, impelled me to take the joint and get high. He knew I was an outsider, not quite a juvenile delinquent, but still not part of the normal crowd. He was lending me his credibility, his cachet, to smooth my transition from special student to part of the herd, the lumpen mass. The effect of the marijuana was to distance me from myself, the miserable me that longed to break free from the undercurrents of sadness and guilt that pulled my family down. It was a fabulously liberating experience.

I smoke John's pot in the box attic of R&R, hidden deep in the ancient stones of Folsom. We debate the relative importance of Jimi Hendrix and Eric Clapton to the history of rock, why jazz is the purest art form, and how the business of smuggling is conducted. I am being recruited because of my thug quality; there's no pretense otherwise. In the shark tank of The Pit, muscle and sharp teeth are necessary. The clear fact that I'm a mercenary, still not committed to any of the big groups, is a strong selling point. I'm also recruited because the tightrope that R&R walks requires a mental dexterity, a certain facility with people, and a high level of cunning. R&R operates on a different playing field from the rest of the joint. We deal with every group; we speak to all parties. This is no small thing in a world where blacks and whites have almost zero interaction. The only exceptions are between the gang leaders and in furtherance of the drug trade—getting high transcends all barriers. We smuggle for all comers, in return for a quarter of what arrives. (The standard deal is to have your contraband in four equal packets in your package—we select which one to keep.) This means we have pounds of pot stored in R&R, secured behind the guards' locks and keys. For the next year, I am stoned every day, and I have so much material wealth it doesn't fit into my cell. I see it as revenge, of a kind. "If the judge could see me now" is a common refrain inside the cells; we're loaded, eating fat burritos, watching television.

Anita comes to visit me a couple of months after I return to Folsom from L.A. County Jail. Her family has mounted a furious and understandable campaign to dissuade her from continuing to see me, including hiring a private investigator and stealing my mail. She arrives at Folsom, looking so beautiful she'll be the subject of conversation on the yard for months to come. I've been visiting a couple of featherwoods, all bad tattoos and twisted intentions. Seeing Anita for the first time without a half-inch-thick plate of shatterproof Plexiglas between us (the county jail allows only non-contact visits), I'm struck by how small she is, how deep her green eyes are, and how soft her skin is under my hands. I kiss her, tasting her, pulling her flush against me. I'm tossed back against the futility of loving a woman so far out of reach, of loving any woman, of love. We talk, we touch, and we part. It's like all visits in prison—too much, in too little time, with too little promise stretched out into the future.

While we're sitting out on the patio, the hulk of Two Building the backdrop, rifle shots crack out through the open windows. The visitors are startled, some scared. We who inhabit this world barely react. I wonder at this, how we prisoners have become so inured to the violence and suffering around us. Anita tells me that, as she approached the prison down the winding road lined with spare trees and sparse grass, she could feel the pain emanating from the place. I still see our isolation as noble, but I sense the way she sees it is more accurate. We only meet one more time at Folsom. I've been found with pot and placed on non-contact visiting status. We visit behind glass. I assume we'll never touch again. It hurts, this conclusion, but it confirms my sense of reality—all good things end poorly.

Our reign in R&R ends in a masterly, if ultimately idiotic, gesture. One of our regular customers has arranged for a pound to be sent in a package. We keep waiting for it to arrive, but nothing shows up. The customer concludes we must have burned him. He's black, we're white—trust is close to impossible between us. He calls home complaining, speaking far too clearly on a monitored phone line. The guards know something is coming in this package. It shows up on the truck a few days later. Our luck is the guard in charge of the process wants the big bust all for himself. It seems, in cop world, the big drug bust is the ultimate badge. He sets the package on top of the big cart we're pushing over to the package annex. We all know this package is hot, too. Ron, the best tattoo artist and toughest convict I have ever known, heads over to the annex and positions himself on the second-story landing. As I push the cart through the door, the overanxious guard focuses all his attention ahead. I reach forward and heave the thirty-pound box straight up into Ron's waiting arms. He slips into one of the rooms, disassembling the box and retrieving the contents. I push the cart over to the package storage room and start unloading. The guard notices the box he was planning to make his bones on is nowhere to be found. He begins a frantic search through the piles of boxes, but he won't tell us what he's looking for. All the while, Ron has distributed the contents throughout the second-floor rooms. I go about my business as usual, collecting a pile of trash to take back out. The guard is apoplectic, but trying to play it off. I ask him to unlock the door so I can take out the trash can, a fifty-gallon drum. He carefully looks through it before turning to put in the big brass key. Ron drops two boxes of Ritz crackers down to me that I shove into the drum. Out the door to our emergency drop point, Billy Marcus in the magazine shack. Within a week, this guard, furious at being so completely snookered out of his big bust, fires all of us for a variety of bogus charges. The move we made becomes the stuff of legends, but I wind up making sandwiches at five in the morning.

I make sandwiches, fill water jugs, and serve food. Months later, the yard clerk's position opens up, a plum assignment. I seek it out, get it, and land back in the mix, even pulling in my closest friend and cellmate as the porter. A perfect assignment. I get out to the yard early, type up a few simple forms, and spend the rest of the day on the iron pile or cruising around the prison. The dynamic is a complex one. The yard lieutenant, a thirty-five-year veteran everyone calls Tex, comes to see me as a sort of son. The rest of the yard guards, who look at Tex as a demigod, treat me with extreme deference. I come and go as I please, showing up for work so stoned I can barely stand up. "Horse, I think you oughta go home," Tex would say, and I'd stumble back to my cell. By this time I'm heavily using drugs—heroin, crank, coke, Dilaudid, Fentanyl, the so-called designer heroin, and the ubiquitous marijuana.

The prison is in the midst of an endless war between the blacks and the Mexicans, while we whites are on our own endless campaign to purify our ranks. For a period of a couple of years, we see twenty to thirty serious stabbings a month. (There were few minor stabbings at Folsom because you would be stabbed for doing a poor job.) Another twenty to thirty guys a month crack under the pressure and check in, seeking protective custody. The viciousness of the place becomes so intense we take bets on whether particular stabbing victims will survive; we set people up for murder with a callousness that defies description; we become so accustomed to all the suffering and pain around us that we stop, I stop, at some essential and fundamental level, being fully human. This is in the midst of era that would be described as a "riot in slow motion." Rifle fire ricochets through the buildings everyday. The sight of guards running by with bleeding victims on gurneys barely raises an eyebrow. Outside the prison, the local ambulance companies line up waiting for the daily carnage, the routine business to come bleeding through the East Gate. The local news announces the weekly and monthly tally—who is winning the race war, how many whites have been dispatched—as a regular feature of the nightly broadcast. Folsom Prison is written up in regional and national publications, touted as the bloodiest joint in America.

As the years roll by, and I grow ever closer to the center of power, a flickering remnant of the delirious, joyful feelings I experienced with Anita lingers. Our letters are sporadic—she's interested, she's not; I'm interested, I'm not. My friend Ron has wisely counseled me to delay joining anything of a "blood in blood out" nature until I'm thirty. My word to him is too important to break.

I waver a couple of times, and I am heavily, regularly recruited, but even at the age of twenty-four I know there is something horribly wrong about that whole scene. The brief injection of humanity and love Anita brought me has undermined my resolve to conquer this patch of the governor's asphalt.

*

The trouble is I've dug myself so deep into The Pit there are no easy ways up and out. In an unexpected twist of fate, all the violence and media attention about the rivers of blood pouring out through the gates, in concert with the new "get tough" mantra of American corrections, results in the first new maximum-security prison built in California in a century. Better still, it is to be sited in the mountains north of Los Angeles, well within reach of Anita. The administration creates a list of candidates, prisoners assumed to be a threat and thus a better bet to open a new joint. I'm not on the list.

Tex, I want to go to the new joint down south. I want to pursue this girl. I can't get her out of my mind.

Do you love her, Horse?

I do, Tex.

Then you should do everything you can to be with her.

How do I get on the list?

I'll do it, but you have to give me your word you won't bring any of this gang crap down there with you. Can you do that?

I stop and think, long and hard. At this prison I'm almost a kingpin; not at the top of the heap, but every day I walk with and get high with and associate with the actual king-pins. I have a perfect job, with a perfect boss, and not a day goes by that I'm not high. Still, that ineffable feeling Anita gives me so carelessly, so easily, won't leave me alone. I want to be loved. It is at this moment that I finally realize this consciously: *I want to be loved.*

I give my word to Tex that I won't bring any "gang crap" to the new prison. Tex and I shake hands. When the final list is announced, I'm on it.

Leaving Folsom is complicated. In a sense, I've grown up amongst the old stones. So much of my identity is wrapped up in the mere fact that I've survived. I wonder how much of me actually *has* survived. My hands are stained blood-red through my involvement in too many terrible things. I can't even count the pieces I've funneled out to the yard that ended up buried in someone's back. My conscience has never bothered me; I have slept well all along. I talk to many of the fellas of my conflicted feelings about leaving The Pit. In private, they all encourage me to get away from this evil place, this evil and pointless life we're living. I'm shocked by their candor. On all their faces, within the confines of their tired and horror-dulled eyes, I see a sadness usually camouflaged in the bloodshot haze of drugs and rage. Junior, one of the most feared of them, tells me he lives a life filled with regrets, that all the violence has been wrong. This is so startling an admission I wonder if it is yet another test. Will I let his brothers know his resolve is faltering? Or would revealing his confidence prove a defect in my character? In this world, at this time, these kinds of decisions can have life-or-death consequences.

I ponder this for days, trying to decide what I should do, what will be the smartest move, the safest move, the move with the least possibility of blowback. But I can't let it go, this denunciation of a way of life I had embraced too easily. One afternoon, back on the iron pile, just the two of us, I finally seek clarification. At first, Junior denies having ever said anything like what I so clearly heard. This man is a living legend in the California prison system. He has stabbed dozens of people. I see him as a kind of negative role model, a bad older brother. But I have tremendous love for him. It was he who first started to casually refer to me as "brother." In the world of the fellas, this is no small thing. He is a large, powerful, and commanding presence, at the peak of his physical and social powers. I'm a young giant, stronger and quicker, perhaps, but nowhere near his overall prowess. I stand my ground and call him on his remorseful soliloquy. Finally, he relents and tells me how badly he wants out of the gang pothole he jumped into. He encourages me to avoid his mistake, to leave Folsom, to abandon my pursuit of false prison glory. In his eyes, I see a flicker of who he must have once been—a loud, rough-around-the-edges young man filled with confidence and zeal—before the blood stained him so ugly.

It's a cold afternoon, late in October of 1985. The granite slab that backdrops the iron pile glistens with moisture. Low clouds slide by, just above the grotesque concrete tower on the hill overlooking the pile. Folsom has been on and off lockdown for the better part of three continuous years. The level of constant violence is unprecedented even in the long, tortured history of The Pit. A weariness has settled over all who walk the yard. Every day another stabbing, another group of potential victims locks up, another load of weapons comes up from the lower yard destined to shorten lives. The ambulances pull up every morning in front of the prison, waiting for it to disgorge the latest casualties.

But these old stones call to me. I, too, feel their bone-weariness. It speaks to the emptiness inside of me. From the first moment I walked into One Building, from the first moment I looked into the depth of the walls, a part of me had felt at home. As the years went on, as I walked through the various buildings, got high in hundred-year-old-granite cells, ate chow under the vast mural in the cavernous Two Dining Hall, as I became a man, I grew to love this horrible place. At night, in the back of One Building, bats come out to chase insects in a stunning aerial ballet. Cats live with and around us, and we adopt some of them. There is a history here, a direct linkage to a real past. Most of us have no direct linkage to much of anything real. I surely don't. Once, I sent a request for three songs to be played on the local rock station: "Hand of Doom" by Black Sabbath, "Sister Morphine" by The Rolling Stones, and "In My Time of Dying" by Led Zeppelin. The words to my request were read over the air with incredulity: "To all who remain free in their hearts." In this prison of prisons, I have felt free—or, more accurately, unconstrained. I have freed the golem of my darkest soul.

Maybe it's the fact that I'm growing older. Maybe, down in my deepest being, I just want to be admired for something good, to be loved, to be wonderful. Whatever the reason, I decide to leave Folsom.

The day before I'm to get on the bus, Tex shakes my hand and wishes me well—he has actual tears in his eyes. Later that night, my cellie and I pack two cut-down cigar tubes with drugs. We push them up our asses an hour before the bus is scheduled to pick us up. While I plan to honor my word and not bring the gang shit with me, I have no intention of going sober, too. We smoke a couple of huge joints minutes before we're strip-searched, placed in waist chains and leg irons, and put on a prison bus.

The bus pulls through the big arch of the West Gate, out through the shadow of the wall, and onto the narrow road leading to the joint. The sides of the road are lined with skinny trees, naked this time of year in the foothills of the Sierra Nevada, the trunks all painted bright white to about six feet up. They remind me of skeletons directing the dead to a decaying mausoleum. As our bus pulls away from the prison, I can almost hear them calling, almost see their skinny fingers clawing at the windows. Folsom doesn't like to give up its adopted children.

California Correctional Institution, Tehachapi: I

I am alone in a holding cell. It's twenty feet deep by eight feet wide, with a porcelain sink and toilet in the back. The solid steel door has a small window; a larger window is in the wall next to it. Wooden benches are bolted to one wall and run the length of the cell. When the medical tech comes to the door, he looks scared. He tells me through the door crack, "You have AIDS." The guard in the booth overlooking the holding cell area, separated from me by two half-inch-thick, shatterproof windows and fifteen feet of space, stands at the far end of his position. Thus begins the two-month ordeal that upsets everything I know about myself and the world I live in.

A year and half earlier, I arrived at the brand new maximum security prison up in the Tehachapi mountains, two hundred miles north of Los Angeles: the California Correctional Institution's Unit IV-A. After Folsom, arriving at this new joint is like leaving the nineteenth century through a tunnel and emerging onto the deck of a spaceship. Nothing is the same. There are no bars, no gun walks, none of the familiar markers that yell at you: *This is prison!* There is no history, no established order, no predictability. The guards are hostile and aggressive. They are determined, in their own words, to take control of this place away from us: "You will run nothing. You will make no decisions. You will comply." The place is designed, seemingly, to minimize any contact between us and them, or perhaps more accurately, to maximize the distance between us and them, and between us and the real world.

Each building holds a hundred and twenty men, less than a full tier of Folsom's One Building, and is further subdivided into three pods of twenty cells each on two tiers. The cells are blessedly large, with a narrow window in the back wall that runs from floor to ceiling. The cell door is solid, with its own small, narrow window. The sink and toilet are stainless steel. There are two lockers and a small metal desk on one long wall, two beds on the other. The walls and ceiling are painted a dull tan. The floor is bare concrete. Each pod has two single-man showers with another solid steel door. The first time I shower, I notice the ceiling in the shower is the shape of a coffin. I also learn the water is controlled from the large, clear-windowed booth that overlooks the pod. Its windows start ten feet from the floor and head up another ten feet to the inside ceiling. They have round ports cut into them through which the barrels of the semiautomatic rifles the booth guards always carry can be aimed. On every free wall are large, red-stenciled admonitions in English and Spanish: No Warning Shots.

Between every other building is a small chow hall that connects the two. Everything is painted the same dull tan— the central tower that stands fifty feet above the small yard, the gym, the industries building, the offices, everything. There is an iron pile and basketball courts, handball courts against a bare concrete wall, and a building that has a chapel at one end and the visiting room at the other. The total population of the facility is less than a thousand, less than just one of the massive blocks up north. There is a claustrophobic quality to this prison, a sense of being trapped in an antiseptic hospital.

When we arrive from Folsom, as we're being off-loaded from the bus, we're met by a phalanx of guards with their batons drawn, poised to fight. All tight-lipped, they won't look us in the face. After the easy banter between guards and convicts we have known and expected all our prison lives, a strict line is drawn that never eases. This is the new, tough-on-crime guard-prisoner dynamic at its inception.

I am singled out from day one. Loud, boisterous, tattooed convicts represent the past that this new approach is designed to stamp out. Fortunately for me, while they assume their fighting stance with admirable resolve, the guards fall woefully short of understanding how this world works. After the initial shock of adjusting to a new environment, we set out to discover the holes in their modern security systems. There are many. In between being searched every few days, having photos of my tattoos taken and retaken, and lifting weights, I spend most of my time high, dealing drugs, and fomenting mild unrest—mostly for sport.

On weekends I enter a different arena, take on a different struggle. Anita comes to visit regularly. Her bright colors and outsize emotions filled the room. We spend hours talking. I have never talked to one person so much before. I learn how she has lived a strangely lonely life, working as a legal secretary and living in her father's house. The weekends she visits with me are her only real outlet. I write her long, detailed letters about all of the things I want to do with her. Increasingly, our visits turn from abstract talk to actual groping and touching. She's admitted to me, embarrassed for some reason I don't at first understand, that she is a virgin. Had I not known her so well, I wouldn't have believed her, but I do. I am determined to be her first. To accomplish this we need to be married in order to qualify for a conjugal visit. I propose. She resists. I make a deal with her: marry me for one year, and if it doesn't work we'll separate, no pain or hostility, just a test drive. This almost works. Finally, after one too many cases of blue balls and wet dreams, I tell her to marry me or move on; I can't take this any longer. The fact that she wants me just as much as I want her, combined with her own impressive stubborn streak, seals the deal.

Serving life without the possibility of parole is a futile experience. It makes all relationships tenuous, limited by the inescapable perimeter, the armed fences and interminable duration of confinement stretching out as far as the mind can conceive. Further actually, because forever is a concept that defies comprehension. At this time, only six years into forever, I find the concept hard to grasp. Even so, I know it is real. Anita doesn't share the sense of impossibility, but she must understand the obvious limitations. We are ruled by the immediacy of our passions.

She comes to see the one-year deal as a chance to consummate our desire, if nothing else. The real sticking point is her deathly fear of AIDS. I haven't hidden from her my intravenous drug use, something she doesn't approve of but accepts as a part of me. As a condition of marrying, she demands I stop using and get tested. The more hysterical voices in the public square are confidently predicting the prison population will be decimated as we all died the ignominious deaths we deserve. The prison system follows its normal approach to crises by ignoring them.

I sign up to see the doctor and ask for the test. He tells me there isn't any test available. I decide to file an appeal. Four weeks later, the administration relents, admitting there is a test and drawing some blood. I am given the standard line: If you don't hear anything in two weeks, the results are favorable. After two weeks, I am told all is well. Two weeks later, over the public address system on the yard, I am directed to report to the clinic. I drop the weights I'm lifting. As I leave the iron pile, I joke about having AIDS and how they're going to lock me up.

*

I've been in this spot, sitting on this wooden bench, for maybe fifteen minutes. This is my greatest test, I tell myself. I will not surrender my dignity. I will not reveal how desperately sad I feel. In some ways, there is poetic justice here. I have never expected to live much past twenty-one; thirty is out of the question. I am twenty-six. I am going to die, soon. But I will not die in this fucking holding cell, on display.

Jimmy Hughes, the prison's X-ray technician, comes out from the back. Shock is stamped on his face. I tell him to go and find Ty, my cellie and closest friend. A few minutes later, Ty stands outside the holding cell, distraught. There is no doubt in either of our minds: we will never see each other again. We have been cellmates for almost three years. You come to know a person in ways far more intimate inside a prison cell than in a marriage. There is a profound and abiding love between us; we're like brothers. He asks me if it's true, and I confirm the message. I will die soon, brother. He breaks down, sobbing, tears pouring down his face. It's as if he's crying for both of us. He desperately wants to hug me, to touch me one last time, but the control booth guard won't open the cell door.

Sergeant Crow shows up in the clinic area. Ty pleads with him to have the door opened. It is one of those too rare moments in prison when humanity triumphs. He orders the door to be opened a few inches. Ty and I shake hands. He looks into my eyes and sees flatness. I have retreated so far into myself I'm not even there. He stumbles back out the door. I learn later that he doesn't come out of our cell for days. The common assumption is that he fears he has AIDS: we shot a lot of dope together. I know better. He is mourning my death, mourning the loss of his best friend.

An hour later two guards show up to transport me to the infirmary on another yard. They're wearing gloves and masks. I am in a van, shackled. As I walk through R&R to the infirmary, there is a wide-open path in front of me. The clerks are standing behind counters, wide-eyed, as a man contaminated by death passes through. I am finally brought to a cell in the infirmary with an ugly red sign already affixed to the outside of the door, my number scrawled across it, the international biohazard symbol prominent. After the door is closed, the handcuffs and shackles are removed. The food port is secured. I am alone.

There is no outside window in this cell, only a skylight that hasn't been cleaned recently. The bed is freestanding, not bolted to the wall; it has a thick mattress. There is a toilet and a sink. No books, no magazines, no radio or television. At Tehachapi, going to the infirmary is a dreaded experience. It's perceived as and is, in fact, punishment. I want a cigarette. I see a male nurse with the outline of a Marlboro box in his shirt pocket. After I catch his attention at the door, I put two fingers to my mouth. He winks. Later, he comes by the door and slips half a dozen smokes and matches to me. I ask him what I should expect next. He tells me all AIDS patients are transferred and isolated in Vacaville, the hospital prison. How long will this take? As soon as someone dies up there and a bed opens up. It shouldn't be too long.

The guards come by with dinner. A paper tray is passed in to me through the port in the door. I notice the guard is nervous, skittish, like he's afraid I'll pull him through the four-inch slot. When he comes back to collect the tray, he's wearing a surgical mask. He puts a red biohazard trash bag up to the slot and directs me to push the tray into it without touching the edge. I come unglued: "Do I look sick to you? Fuck you and your bag!" He steps back and starts to bluster the routine threats, including "We'll come in there and kick your ass." I dare him. We both know his deathly fear of being infected greatly outweighs his desire to take any punitive actions. He slams the port shut with a mighty thrust and stalks off. I'm juiced with a thousand volts of rage. In the next hour, I launch into a frenzied workout until I'm exhausted and dripping with sweat. I birdbath in the sink, smoke a cigarette, and lie on the fat, cushy rack. Hours later, in the dead quiet of the night, I fall to the ground and sob, crying until I'm emptied of emotion. I keep repeating, searching at first, angry for a while, and plaintive at the end, Why me? The answer comes back to me from out of the void: Because you are a rotten son of a bitch.

In the next few days, I live through an experience more surreal than usual for prison, and prison is fundamentally surreal. At first, I'm not allowed to use the phone. When I finally am, I'm directed not to tell whomever I call why I'm in the infirmary or the line will be cut. Anita calls the prison and is told she can only visit me behind glass. When she arrives, she is told she can't see me at all. She asks the chaplain to let me know she was there. She also asks a redneck sergeant the same thing. Only the sergeant shows up, looking like he's walking into a radioactive chamber. Ultimately, four days into it, I'm shackled and put into a van with a very sick black guy, driven three hundred miles by two guards who never remove their surgical masks, and delivered to Vacaville.

California Medical Facility, Vacaville

The intake unit for AIDS patients is a small, eight-man dorm filled with homosexuals. After another series of blood tests, and a prescient admonition not to shoot dope lest I be infected with more than one strain of the virus, I am moved to L wing on the first floor, where all the unfortunates of the California prison system known to be infected are quarantined. The unit is composed of three parts. The cells, which are bigger than Folsom's and smaller than Tehachapi's, are situated down a hallway, each side about twenty cells long, the last two on each side behind a grill gate for lockup and segregation purposes. The dayroom area doubles as a chow hall since the rest of the prisoners have filed a mass petition demanding that AIDS cases be banned from the common chow hall. The yard area sits in the space between L wing and the next wing, with a high concertina-wire, chain-link fence at the end. Trash and abuse rain down from the floors above L-1.

In the space of one week, I have migrated from the upper echelon of the prisoner caste system down to a sub-basement. I'm surrounded by the outcasts of the outcast. It's a humbling moment. I quickly realize how I would view myself, were I on the other side of the door to the AIDS unit. In the little world of prison I will be smutted up mercilessly. The line will be that I was always gay. AIDS is viewed as a gay man's disease, no less inside than out. Homosexuality, while not generally viewed as grounds for banishment, is grounds for the loss of all serious respect in the joint. A dicksucker can never be a leader or seen as a stand-up guy.

Somehow, for maybe the first time in my life, I become sensitive to the terrible disrespect others around me have had to endure. Being stained, I see the stain for what it is, and I find myself listening to the desperate stories of others with a new attention. My cellmate tells me he plans to inject himself with bleach because bleach kills the virus. The most affecting thing I hear, constantly, is how these men have contracted a deadly disease by doing what is natural for them. When I relate my rationale for getting tested, what had been an essentially pragmatic decision to have sex becomes noble, heroic even. I was protecting the woman I loved. At a mandatory group orientation, a young psychologist tells me she is impressed by how well I'm adjusting. I go to one of the cells where an inmate is in full-blown disintegration, a frail vestige of his former self. I see my future shivering under a pile of blankets in an empty prison cell. I vow to fight to the end, not out of vainglory, but out of a stubborn refusal to knuckle under.

Two weeks into living consciously with AIDS, I'm fully committed to a new, pared-down ambition, that of survival and health. I tell people I will be one of those rare individuals who never get sick, and more than one person believes me, I think. More important, I believe me. I am not caught up in some denial of reality. I am turning the lessons of my life, of being indomitable and unafraid, toward a new challenge. I also feel the first stirrings of a kind of protective impulse. Through a broken window in the corridor, some of my fellow prisoners attempt to purchase drugs from the mainline prisoners. They're burned about half the time. While being escorted down the corridor one day, I recognize one of these unscrupulous dealers. As I pass him by, I whisper, "You best make good or I'll break you in two the next time I see you, pigs around or not." We lock eyes for a second before he breaks weak. The next day, he's at the window with a fair deal.

I'm in the little side room used for doctor visits. The doctor tells me there's a problem with my tests.

What does that mean, a problem?

The test is inconclusive.

What does inconclusive mean?

It's negative, we think.

I was told two tests were done at Tehachapi, and both were positive.

There's no record of a second test. We will schedule you for a Western blot, the gold standard, as soon as possible.

No, doctor, you will order that test right now.

He sees the anger coloring my face. Up to this point, I had assumed medical personnel operated differently from the rest of the prison system. It's clear to me now they don't. I'm escorted up to the lab for the next series of tests. During the past two weeks, I have spoken with Anita several times on the phone. She is devastated, drinking too much, and feeling somehow guilty for all of this, as if requesting the test has given me AIDS. I console her and tell her that she has allowed me to do one truly right thing in my life: protecting her from something terrible. I encourage her to move on. Whatever we thought we would have is now over. I sort of mean it. It's always in the darkest moments that a person's true character reveals itself. Anita's actions during this period do more to change my view of human beings than I would have believed possible. She starts calling the prison to find out how she can still marry me. The prison officials tell her I can't marry anyone now, but her naive efforts touch me profoundly. From my perspective, cultivated over years of living in a world of selfish grasping, what she is now doing simply doesn't add up. It's all the more remarkable in light of her deep fear of illness. She makes a decision based on the urging of the best part of herself, something I have so rarely seen, something I have so rarely done myself.

The next seven days drip by. I have a close friend, BG, who is carrying on a clandestine affair with one of the medical techs. I get at her for the news. She tells me, all serious-faced and solicitous, it came back positive. This is the definitive test. You have AIDS. You will probably die within a year. I'm sorry.

I get myself moved into a single cell and start the process of fixing it up. The next week, I'm painting, polishing, acquiring the stuff I need to live with a semblance of comfort. By the end of the week, my cell is now my house. The walls are clean and shining. The floor glows with several coats of wax. This is an action I've learned over a lifetime in Mother California's jails and prisons. There are two fundamental choices in doing time: One is a passive approach that renders the prisoner a victim of fate, as manifested in prisoners who wear ill-fitting state clothes and live in beat-up cells. Those who deal with imprisonment this way will argue they are simply refusing to give in and accept their confinement. The other approach is to become active, to clean up your surroundings and your clothes. By standing up and taking charge of yourself, you influence and create your environment. Your cell is your home. For the defeated, their cell is a cage they flail around in, forever reminding themselves how dismal their lives are.

After another week, I'm in the doctor's office. The test result is negative. I don't have AIDS. The medical tech who told me the opposite a week earlier is standing behind the doctor. She shrugs her shoulders and looks away when I try to pin her eyes. She says the prevalent feeling is that anyone who asks for the test must have it. Then she asks me if I've done anything in here that could have exposed me to the virus. For weeks I've done nothing but figure out how to deal with this, how to adjust to a wholly, wildly different reality. In this adjustment, for once in my life, I have stayed sober. No shooting dope. Sex never entered my mind. After I tell her I've done nothing that could have exposed me, she tells me I'm being released today.

It is a joyous moment tempered by the fact I'm placed in the hole. Before I leave the AIDS unit, I'm surrounded by the sad denizens of this terrible place. Many hugs, many handshakes, and I'm out the door. I don't realize I'm heading to the hole until I'm inside the front door of the unit. T wing, administrative segregation overflow, a unit that is completely devoid of programs. No yard, no canteen, no phones, nothing. I understand the reasoning, as I'm considered something of a super-thug and the main line of Vacaville is a soft medical facility. But the conditions are atrocious, nonetheless. The cell is an over-under, which means one cell has the upper bunk and the adjacent cell the lower bunk set into the dividing wall. The rest of the cell is tiny, just enough room for a toilet-and-sink combo. On the back wall is a large window broken into sixteen little windows by steel mullions. My view is of the parking lot and the perimeter road. Inside, the wing is designed much like it is at Soledad—three open tiers with large, steel staircases at the front and the back. My cell is on the second tier, the last on one side.

It is now Thursday. I arrived in the hole on Monday. The rules require a seventy-two-hour review of all administrative segregation placements. It's called a 114 hearing because that's the number on the form. I am in handcuffs, sitting in front of Lieutenant Rey, a guard I knew at Folsom. He tells me there is a problem with my AIDS tests. I am actually positive, but the medical department doesn't want to deal with me. He says he will have all the paperwork for me by tomorrow, this coming Monday, at the latest. He is compassionate, fatherly almost. Back to the tiny cell. In four weeks, I have been told three times that I have AIDS three times, and twice that I don't.

Friday comes and goes with no paperwork. Monday is the same. Mondays pass by until I have been in the hole for a month with no human contact save the manacled walk to the shower. I have no property, no reading material, no television or radio, nothing to distract me from the forced consideration of my life. It doesn't start well because the

AIDS issue consumes me. For a solid week, maybe two—time dilates and contracts on me—my stoic calm disintegrates. I begin a ritualized examination of lymph node sites, followed by trying to peer into the back of my throat in the few square inches of cracked mirror left on the wall above the sink.

I start at the back of my jawline, sinking the tips of my fingers in deep, exploring for the telltale hard nodules. I feel the rubbery tubes of veins and arteries, like small engine hoses. Moving my fingers forward, I trace the outline of my jawbone, working all around it, pressing till my fingertips push against the fibrous musculature of my tongue. After working over this area a couple of times—there always seem to be hard spots, something worth another rooting—I move down to my collarbone, probing around the surprisingly delicate structure, its frail quality out of place with its central location. I try to work around the back, seeking the string of pearls indicative of disease. Next, it's the armpits, pushing in all the angles, feeling my ribs. Finally, after I've worked my way into a foul, fearful sweat, I am digging around my groin. This is the toughest area to push through the armature I have spent the past ten years developing. It is my nature to do everything roughly, in a heavy-handed way, and this self-examination is no different. By the time I run out of steam, I'm bruised and swollen, the back of my throat hurts from overextending my tongue, and my hands are sore from inflicting so much punishment. I am, at every level of my being, spent.

The letters I'm receiving from Anita grow increasingly desperate and remorseful. She continues to believe all of this is her fault. She's confused and frightened. She's called the prison to inquire why she hasn't heard from me. In the last letter she received before I ran out of paper and envelopes, I told her I was in the hole, that I was infected, and I hadn't been seen by a doctor or anyone else. She is told that I'm not in the hole, I'm in the hospital. She shouldn't believe anything I tell her because people as sick as I am lie; AIDS affects the brain first.

I have a terminal illness, but I have no symptoms. I'm not in the hospital or the AIDS wing, but everyone confirmed to be positive must be isolated in one of those units. Every kite (what we call a note) I send to medical goes unanswered. Every kite I send to the lieutenant who ordered this placement goes similarly unanswered. I have never seen with my own eyes any of these tests, positive or negative. I'm dirty and hungry. It has been weeks since I've achieved the complete release of sleep, a sleep uninterrupted by violent intrusions. I close my eyes and let go of the drama playing out in my mind. Every part of my body hurts, but in deep, healing breaths that pour out of me in a torrent, I blow out the pain. Burrowing deeper into myself, I cross a threshold beyond which I feel an abyss, a great emptiness. I teeter on the edge of this void. I keep breathing. Finally, I give up the struggle. I tumble downward, spinning wildly. I'm dizzy. There is no bottom. Down, down past fear, down past ego, down past desire. Then, like a diver who reaches equilibrium in the depths, I float weightless. This is death.

When I return to full awareness of my circumstances, still alone in an ugly prison cell, still unsure of my health, still unable to do a damned thing about any of it, I feel less fear and less rage. I see the shimmering, blue summer sky. I hear the ravens marching around on the parched grass, hollering out to one another, hopping up into the air spreading their fabulous ink-black wings. I stare out of the window for a long while before I lie down to sleep.

In the next week I wake early, before the clanging, braying fury of this hole fills the air. I sit down on the floor and let go, falling to deeper depths each time. I don't pray or beg or chant mantras to good health. I simply release my grip on the conscious world around me. Each time I throw myself off that precipice, I come back feeling less burdened, lighter, less weighed down. I know in some part of myself that communicates without words that I'm getting closer to the place I need to get to.

I'm floating in the warmth of honey, thick sweetness all around me, a gentle pressure like a tender hug. This is the place I've been groping toward over the past week. There is connection of a kind I have never experienced or imagined. Tendrils of light explode away from me in every direction, shooting off into a space crowded with innumerable rays and specks and filaments. It's as if everything is connected to me. Wondering whether I'm infected, I realize it doesn't matter, not really. Wherever I look the view is the same. Nothing is apart from me. There is no anger here. There is no fear.

For how long this goes on, I don't know. When I return to my cell, it is different. I sit on the edge of the bed tossing crumbs onto the outside of the windowsill. The pigeons come and jostle for a space to eat. I walk over to the sink and splash water on my face and smooth out my hair. After drying myself, I notice something on my right shoulder and brush it off, slapping my shirt. One of the pigeons flies into my cell and lands on my shoulder. It's stunning and unexpected, so startling for a moment that I think I'm dreaming or imagining it. I pick the bird up and set it back on the windowsill, walk over to the sink, and slap my shoulder again. A flurry of feathers and a rush of air and there's the bird on my shoulder. For the next hour, I'm a boy playing with a new pet. Lost completely in the moment, in the present. AIDS, prison, marriage, reputation, sadness—all of it is thoroughly dissolved and gone. More fundamentally, for the first time in a dark city block I feel joy. I laugh out loud at this incongruous situation, at this ungainly bird, at the knot of tension and fear I have become.

I don't name my companion. (I've always thought the naming of animals presumptuous.) Nor do I try to capture it for my pleasure or solace. It comes and goes through the broken window unimpeded. It stays for an hour, give or take, once or twice a day, over the next week or ten days. It doesn't fear me. There is something beyond categorization, beyond naming, that extends from my suffering and connects to this bird. How I know this will always be one of the most perplexing mysteries of my life.

Thus fortified by my journey into myself, and by some sort of miraculous intervention, I decide it's time to take a stand. For too long I have been a passive victim, not a stalwart son of Mother California. At my next tier time, I exit the cell with my mattress over my shoulder. I walk to the back of the building, hang the mattress over the railing, and take a few deep breaths. I'm not angry. I'm determined. Back to the front, up to the locked grill gate. I tell the guard he must produce a medical person with my file, or we will be fighting back all the way back to my cell. I remind him I have AIDS; I will bite and spit. This particular guard is a decent sort. He'll call medical. He comes back from the phone. "I give you my word I will get someone from medical over here, but please lock up for now," he tells me. I go back to my cell. For whatever reason, I believe him. An hour later, a senior medical technician stands in the doorway to my cell, showing me my chart. The final test, a Western blot, is noted "negative." There is no doubt, no confusion, and no way anyone could interpret the results as anything but negative.

In the past two months, I have been told three times that I have AIDS, and three times that I don't have AIDS. I have also experienced being part of the lesser caste of prisoners. It's a painful and uncomfortable taste of living outside the power structure. I don't like it a bit. But during these couple of months, I've been exposed to a group of men I normally wouldn't have given the time of day.

When I had first arrived at the AIDS wing, I was alone. Alone in a way to which I was not accustomed. This used to be a relatively small fraternity, a band of brothers, Mother California's bastard sons. Once admitted to the crooked circle, anywhere you went you were always among friends, of a sort. Arriving at a new joint, you would be sought out by your fellow regulars. Where you coming from? Do you know this guy or that guy? By the end of the day, after playing the "Do you know?" game, you were granted conditional acceptance to whichever group you aspired to join. Ever since I first stood on the lush, green grass of Los

Padrinos Juvenile Hall, amid the raucous cries of peacocks, my gray sweatshirt stamped L.A. COUNTY, I had stood with the hardheads and hard cases. My credentials were impeccable and untarnished. I knew almost everybody worth knowing.

A day or two after I arrive in L-1 the guard calls out my name, telling me I have a visitor. I walk up expecting to see one of the usual tattooed roughnecks. Instead, the little bald man who walked up to me in his purple briefs on the fellas' yard, Millie, is standing there with a grocery bag of goodies. He tells me how sorry he is to hear of my plight, and if I need anything else to let him know. Another day or two later, Sunshine, a well liked guy who works in the laundry, shows up with some decent clothes to offer me. More commiseration. More reassurances.

Perhaps most surprising, a week or so later, Bobby Butler shows up on our little yard off the main line. He's in his late fifties, a tall, trim, silver-haired old convict who just happens to be one of the original fellas. He is also a former fella. This is a complicated thing, as former fellas tend to be highly disfavored, one could even say hated. Blood in blood out. At this point in my life, there are still those who mistakenly think I was closer to the tip than I was. He introduces himself, tells me he knows who I am, puts an arm on my shoulder, and lets me feel he's there for me. "What do you need, youngster?"

Vacaville is a relatively soft yard with a higher than normal prevalence of gays and older guys, but because it's also a medical facility there are "regulars" on the yard. I recognize a few of them walking down the central corridor under escort. They wave, but not much more. The gay plague simply isn't a reputation enhancer.

Now that I've pressed the issue of my AIDS status, I'm brought to a committee hearing. The decision they've reached before I'm escorted into the room is not to transfer me back to Tehachapi. Up and down the prison system, the AIDS hysteria has infected prisoners no less than those who live in the real world. Prisoners have filed petitions to isolate all those suspected of being infected, to remove all homosexuals from mainline prisons, and to enact ludicrous and punitive general restrictions. I strenuously object. If I'm moved, for the rest of my natural life in prison it will be assumed that I have AIDS. I must go back to the yard I left to reclaim my life. Probably due to their confusion and, maybe even a moment of humanity, the committee reverses its decision and orders me back to Tehachapi. I'm the first man in the prison system to be cured of AIDS.

I leave in a van sitting next to a dying man who is escorted by guards with surgical masks.

California Correctional Institution, Tehachapi: II

I'm back on fish row at Tehachapi. Within a couple of weeks, I have my old job, my old cell, my old slot on the iron pile, and my old cellmate back. The force field around me is supercharged. Everyone thinks I have AIDS.

Despite—or maybe because of—all we've been through, my relationship with Anita has deepened and assumed a level of intensity that is almost frightening. Our first visit after I return is charged with emotion. Anita feels connected to me through my sacrifice. More than ever before, I see in her the path out of the barrens of my inner life.

One of my earliest childhood memories goes back to when we were living in Brooklyn. Every night my younger brother and I would wait for the fireworks over Coney Island. From our bedroom window, the exploding colors seemed painted on the night sky. We would wrestle around the room. I would let him win some of the matches. My father would inevitably come stomping up the stairs, pulling his skinny leather belt out. "All right you two birds," he would say, "turn over." We would assume the spanking position and receive our licks until we cried out in pain. Then he would order us to go back to our beds, warning us not to make him come up here again. As soon as he left, we would be giggling under our blankets. It was a ritual. At least in those few moments we had his attention.

I have an earlier memory. I'm sitting at the top of the stairs. I can hear my mother and father arguing downstairs through the flickering blue light flooding the hallway. I have a pillow across my knees. I'm coughing deeply into the pillow, muffling the sound. I'm torn between hiding the fact that I'm sick and breaking into the mighty struggle in the living room. My mother suddenly appears at the foot of the stairs. She is still young and wasp-waisted, a tall, beautiful woman whose tangle of black hair and green eyes radiate a vital energy. She asks me why I'm sitting there and I bark out a full-body cough in reply. She asks me if I'm sick. "Yes," I say, coughing out the word. Then she asks me why I didn't tell her. "I was afraid you would throw me away." Those are my words, I'm certain. It's my voice, smaller and more tentative, but mine all the same. After that, the clarity of memory fades into a hospital bed, double pneumonia, and my desperate desire to have my stuffed animals, especially "Doggy-bear." For the life of me, I can't be certain if I ever got them or not. When I'm feeling more generous to my parents, I recall that I did. When I am less charitable to their ghosts, I'm sure I lay in that bed recovering without the comfort of my favorite stuffed friends. But my forlorn words reverberate to this day.

*

The wedding is a simple ceremony in the visiting room, attended by Anita's oldest brother and my prisoner friends Ty and Mike Maloney, in late October of 1987, a little more than half a year after my return from the dead. The minister is an ex-con, a wide Mexican fellow with a salt-and-pepper mustache. He says the words that carry the weight of centuries of tradition, the majesty of love and commitment, of faith and endurance. The same words couples pledge every day in thousands of such ceremonies. But inside the confines of a prison visiting room with a twenty-foot-high ceiling and stark walls, they seem out of place, in a language foreign to this world. When we first kiss as husband and wife, I pull Anita to me and dive into her with a fierce passion.

A month later, we're in the family visiting apartment. The little unit sits inside a tall, razor-wired enclosure out behind the main kitchen gate under the imposing shadow of a perimeter tower. Behind the tower a hill pushes up and away, dotted by scrub trees and exposed rocks. There are patches of snow on the ground. In front of the apartment is a denuded expanse of about fifty yards before the low buildings start, their facades fenestrated by the regular array of cell windows. My cell is almost in view, just around one of the points. Inside the apartment are two bedrooms, a bathroom, a living room, and a small walk-in kitchen. I carry Anita over the threshold to the forty-four hours we will have together. Over the following two days, I learn she truly was a virgin, and how humanizing it is to be with a woman again without the ever-present stares of prison guards.

I also discover the utter depression of returning to prison after she leaves. Once Anita is processed out and I clean up the apartment, after performing the ritual-ized strip search, I'm escorted back through the large gate and then an inner gate to the upper yard. This is the first of the many times I make the long walk back to my cell. The bare yard looks particularly confining. The central tower looks taller and more menacing. The front steel door to the housing unit seems thicker and louder crashing closed behind me. My cell feels less like my house and more like the cage it is, no matter my efforts to soften its concrete edges, to claim it away from the system. I have never done harder time.

Unlike Folsom, which, for all its ferocity and granite-tinged darkness, always allowed for the free expression of personality inside our cells, Tehachapi is hell-bent on maintaining an atmosphere of sterility; there's a dull sameness to everything. My last cell at Folsom had a white ceiling, sand-tan walls of high-gloss paint, a brick-red floor polished with many coats of wax, and chocolate-brown highlights on the lockers and bed frames. There were several Maxfield Parrish paintings in redwood frames behind glass, and numerous hooks of burnished brass. We even had handmade bedspreads in complementary colors. Tehachapi forbids anything on the walls—not a painting, not a poster, not a photograph. The walls and ceiling, the lockers and bed frames, are all the same washed-out tan. The floor is bare concrete. In the five years I spent up north my cell was never searched. This new joint compels the guards to search us constantly. The policy stems from their operating ethos—to remain in charge of every facet of our lives.

In the time since returning from Vacaville, after the multiple contradictory pronouncements on my AIDS status, I have become obsessed with my health. The truth of it is I've turned into a bit of a hypochondriac. I develop a hardcore health regimen. I no longer use intravenous drugs, which seems logical in light of the recent past. I quit smoking, and ramp up my workout routine. The trouble is I feel I need to be on constant guard against losing weight. Haunted by the barely living skeletons at Vacaville, I grow giant-sized, spending hours on the iron pile building a fortress to protect me from the ravages of an illness I never had.

Embarked on my inner journey to self-awareness, I start reading every book I can find about personal growth. Although I was raised a Catholic, at least nominally, the memories of my mother's bitter tears at the moment of consecration of the host keep me away from the religion of my youth. She had been excommunicated after divorcing her Catholic first husband and marrying my Protestant father. Bo Lozoff's *We're All Doing Time*, aimed primarily at prisoners but positing the commonality of our life experience, stands out as one of the first books to speak to me with clarity. I'm particularly moved by his simple lessons regarding meditation. Follow the breath, in and out, works for me much more effectively than grand dissertations on the cosmic connections of Eastern mysticism.

I'm standing on the yard at Tehachapi. It's a cold morning in the winter of 1989. The yard is, as always, visibly divided into the three large groups of California's prisons—whites, blacks, and Mexicans. For the past several months I have been jogging, or rather slogging, around the dirt track. I'm overweight and slow, embarrassingly slow. Running has never been my thing; I'm too big for it. Nevertheless, I've been trying. Petee Wheatstraw, a black guy from Watts, powers by, his effortless stride a mockery of my lurching gait. I pull in behind him and try to pace him for a lap or two. I'm back about ten yards. Whites and blacks don't run together, ever. He notices me and slows down enough for me to stay with him. I last a couple of laps longer than usual. As I pull off the track he returns to his normal pace. For the next month, I regularly pull in behind him and he slows enough for me to keep up. One day I'm behind by only a couple of yards. Straw, I want to make two miles today. He slows a little more and we're side by side. I make the distance. For the next three years that I'm on this yard, we run together. Straw and I are both regulars, both solid members of the harder edge of our respective groups. Our running around the track together every afternoon for years sends a powerful message. This is one of the formative experiences of my life. The two of us would never have spoken to one another or crossed the barrier if we had waited for a peace treaty or an invitation.

Equally important, if not more so, I learn that acts such as this give permission to others to abandon their tacit apartheid. In his masterwork, *Man's Search for Meaning*, Viktor Frankl talks about how in the worst of situations each person retains the ability to control his own inner state. All my life I have felt caught in reaction to forces out of my control. The truth is, these forces are out of my control, but I am in control of myself. For a prisoner, this is a realization of immense proportions. It's too easy to slip into the raging chasm of reaction, a dark place I've spent too much time in myself. Luckily for me, Mother California's minions decide to push me further down the path to awakening.

The memo on the dayroom wall reads: "In thirty days random drug testing will begin. Refusing to submit a urine sample for testing will constitute a positive test. Loss of visiting privileges will be enforced." I immediately know two things: though the policy is clearly outside the bounds of the rules, it will be enforced, and I will be in the first random group to be tested. I walk back to my cell. The Los Angeles Rams are playing the San Francisco 49ers on Monday Night Football. I have a fat joint I'm planning to smoke during halftime. For the past couple of years I have gradually moved away from drugs. Pot is the last remaining vestige of my previous life as a committed user. I smoke this last delicious joint and tell my cellie I'm done with all drugs. This leads to one of the more memorable of arguments in my entire life. Ty is livid. He is trapped in the irrational state of reaction we all tend to inhabit in prison. After trying to convince me I should continue getting high, that I should return to shooting dope with him, and my telling him I couldn't afford to lose my visits, he blurts out, "Is the pussy that good?" Yes, it is that good. He is so disgusted he climbs up on his bunk, faces the wall, and goes to sleep. I never get high again.

In keeping with my new, sober approach to life, I join the AA/NA group. It's an illuminating experience on many levels. I'm astounded by the level of bullshit pouring out of my fellow prisoners. Men I know to be regular users march into the monthly meetings, stand in front of the group, and blather on and on about how they've found the light of the clean life. It's dispiriting. At the very least, I've been direct, and blatant lying just to ingratiate themselves with a couple of old drunks (as they describe themselves) who volunteer their time feels immediately wrong. Delving deeper into myself, I discover that the world looks a lot different through eyes not besotted and addled. It turns out I have lived a life of selfish pleasure-seeking that has brought me little pleasure, and has stolen the pleasure of too many others. The selfishness is painfully clear.

I've even been willing to put Anita at risk. After our first couple of conjugal visits, I bring out some pot. She has never gotten high before. We retreat to the bathroom of the apartment where there is an exhaust fan. I roll us a joint and pass it to her. A few minutes later, she is red-eyed and grinning. I ask her if she now understands why I want her to bring me some. Of course she agrees to do it; she is stoned. Before the end of the visit I get a promise from her to smuggle some in at our next regular visit, with detailed instructions on the correct procedures.

A couple of weeks later, I'm sitting in the visiting room, waiting for Anita. After we kiss and exchange pleasantries, I ask Anita if she has the balloons. She does, but she asks me if I'm really going to make her do this. I remind her how she gave me her word. Then, in a complicated maneuver that involves a can of soda, a bag of peanut M&M's, and megawatts of nervous energy, she passes me eleven balloons. Because I'm sitting in the middle of the room, directly in front of the guard station, I elect to swallow them. After considerable choking and gulping of Coca-Cola, I get them down, to be retrieved the next day. I tell Anita when I've swallowed all eleven, but she claims she gave me twelve. I argue she only gave me eleven, but she insists she gave me twelve. We go back and forth for a good while. I look around me, checking for the third and fourth time all the containers used in the process, and conclude the poor girl simply miscounted. This is not good. It's a felony for which she could serve time. I'm so consumed by my furious desires, by my need to escape myself, this possibility never enters my mind. At the regular time, close custody count is announced. Those of us considered a higher risk to escape have to be counted an extra couple of times every day. I walk up to the guards' station to check in. On my way back to the table, I see a shiny red balloon sitting directly on the floor under my chair. My heart skips a few beats. Mustering all of my self-control, I stoop to the ground as if to tie my shoe and snatch the missing dope. After much struggle, I force it down my throat. It takes a week of digging in my own shit before they finally appear, all bloated and bleached. And, yes, I smoke the dope with much gusto.

At the bottom of my journey of self-discovery in the twelve-step arena, I find the first substantial flickering of pride based on my ability to make a rational, positive decision. It is out of this, more than anything else, that I'm compelled to speak, to tell my story. I always start my testimonial with, "I am a recovering alcoholic, addict, and asshole. Of the three, the last is my worst habit." It always gets a laugh. I come to believe that I have to purge myself of the poison I have worked so assiduously to accumulate, so I talk in the forum of AA/NA. But I don't just talk, I start to reformulate who I am, who I should be, who I want to be. Most of my fellow prisoners don't grasp the sincerity of what I'm saying, hearing only a polished thug's rap. A few get it and tell me privately they are moved and inspired. But all the old drunks hear exactly what I'm saying. I'm talking myself out of the hole I dug myself into over the past fifteen years of my life. I recognize how much I've allowed my hurts and bruises and complaints to turn me into the "feverish, selfish little clod" George Bernard Shaw described in *Man and Superman*, "complaining that the world will not devote itself to making you happy."

During this period of my life, I begin reading seriously, in a more focused way. Books had always been a part of my life; my mother taught me to read before I went to elementary school. She had the astonishing ability to read a long book straight through in one sitting. I read every volume of the *World Book Encyclopedia* that my great-grandmother sent us. Before I climbed out my bedroom window and ran from all I felt, I would spend hours on end by myself. I read prodigiously as a boy, preferring the company of books to others: college textbooks, histories of everything, biographies, science treatises, and philosophy. But I never read with purpose.

I try to read more systematically now. Having no formal training, I struggle to grasp the arcane language of Kant and Camus, and the favorite philosopher of prisoners, Nietzsche. Reading Will and Ariel Durant's *The Story of Philosophy*, I come to the conclusion that I'm a stoic, which I read to mean more than simply stone-faced. The idea is to achieve equanimity, to drive disorder out of my life. Stoicism emphasizes the taking of personal responsibility—a character trait and a way of life completely foreign to the world of prison.

To add to this heady mix of intoxicants, I start group therapy with a remarkable shrink: Dr. Haskett, recently hired to deal with the constant collapse of the minds and wills of prisoners. Being in the joint heaves a lot of weight onto your back: the isolation from family and friends, the constant threat of violence, the noise and chaos, the guilt. In any good-sized institution, nearly every day someone cracks apart; it is a fact of this life. Observed decompensation, as the psychiatrists call it—coming apart, as we call it—is yet another pressures of prison life. Prison guards tend to assume all such episodes are feigned to secure more favorable treatment, and though some are, most are not. Someone has to be around to weed out the malingerers from the genuinely broken.

In the course of his duties, Dr. Haskett passes by the door to my office where I sit typing reports and listening to music. Each time he walks by, I start up a conversation and, ultimately, suggest he form a lifer's group. One day he stays and asks me to get him some names. Thus begin the four years of my participation in group therapy with four other men. Guided by a talented professional, we are able to develop a level of trust, to delve more deeply into ourselves, than I could ever have imagined possible. I have lived with my fears of abandonment and ostracism all my conscious life, but I could never label and own these feelings. The other men in the group are as profoundly affected as I am. At different times, we all cry, we all reveal parts of ourselves not usually opened in the predatory world of prison, and we grow.

Never before have I been able to put a name to those I victimized. Thomas Allen Fellowes was always, merely, the victim. As a consequence of the group therapy, the twelve-step process, the books I'm reading, and the incalculable effect of the love I feel from Anita—all of this part of the internal journey to master myself—I'm determined to rehumanize the man I killed. This is particularly difficult, as I only knew Mr. Fellowes for a few minutes before I killed him. Somehow, in some vague and wholly indefinable way, I come to believe that he still exists through me. I'm determined to remake myself, as it's the only possible way I can even begin to atone for stealing his life.

*

While Tehachapi is several orders of magnitude less violent and less brutal than Folsom, it has its peculiar cruelties. The guards have a so-called hands-on policy, which translates into the regular beating of prisoners. In their devoted pursuit of remaining in control, or at least maintaining the illusion of it, the guards mutate into the most intrusive and hostile I have ever seen. This is the beginning of the institutionalized program to strip away our humanity. It coincides with the societal turn away from rehabilitation toward punishment for the sake of inflicting pain. The guards at Tehachapi didn't need much urging to adopt this approach—it fit like a pair of old, well-oiled handcuffs.

The apotheosis of this approach is the "no warning shot" policy. Traditionally, in California prisons, unless a guard is being attacked, the first shot from the rifles will be a warning to desist. Usually there are multiple warning shots, as the guards have no real desire to shoot anyone. The rationale proffered for the change in policy has something to do with the nature of the newly designed prisons. All the concrete and angles would result in ricochets all over the place. None of us pay much attention to the matter until guys start getting shot to death for being involved in stabbings, with the victims of the incidents as likely to be shot as the assailants. It gets worse when fistfights become a viable and justifiable reason to open fire. Being killed for fighting with another man, an almost unavoidable part of the prison experience, strikes all of us as madness.

A good friend named John S. files a civil rights complaint against the policy of wanton shooting. A hearing is convened before a federal magistrate in the Facility-A visiting room, and John asks me to testify about medical procedures. My AIDS experience qualifies me, I suppose, and I have begun to get interested in the legal issues surrounding the prison system. I have fallen under the same misapprehension of reality as the Russian peasants being brutalized by the Cossacks. If only the Tsar knew, he would put a stop to this madness. Of course, the Cossacks worked for the Tsar, and the courts are no less a part of the government than the prison system itself. My zeal for justice would prove my undoing.

I'm escorted into a small hearing room off of the main visiting room. At the center of the room, behind a wide, oak table, sits a black-robed federal judge. Along one side sits the platoon of deputy attorneys general and a court reporter; on the other side sits John, representing himself. Positioned across the back wall are several prison officials, including our program administrator, Mr. V, who epitomizes the short-man complex about as well as any short man I've ever met. He wears a black suit with a black shirt and a black tie, and black shoes with a little extra at the heel. His black trench coat seals the mafioso look. Although I'm sure he imagines he exudes menace, to all of us, and to most of his staff, he looks like what I suspect he really is—a little man playing tough guy. We already dislike each other. No matter how hard I've tried to break this pattern, over the course of my life, small men have tended not to like me.

The judge asks me a series of questions related to medical care and the provision of medical services. It's pretty routine stuff. How long does it take you to see the doctor, and so on. Almost as an afterthought, the judge asks me if we are ever forced to wait outside in the rain or snow for medications. Tehachapi is almost five thousand feet up in the mountains north of Los Angeles County; it snows every winter and often in the spring and fall. It also rains—fat, high-elevation drops driven sideways by the mountain winds. The get-tough guards make it a point to have us wait outside in the pill line, weather be damned. He looks puzzled, and follows up by asking if this occurs regularly. Truthfully and without hesitation, I tell him it's been happening ever since this place opened. Then he asks me how I'd respond if he told to me that an official of this prison testified, under oath that inmates are never made to wait outside for medication during foul weather. I tell him whoever testified to that is a liar. I sense a tightening in the row of officials. Mr. V's face is aflame with anger. I know right then he is the liar, which is confirmed to me later. Within a few weeks, a couple of months at most, I'm in the hole.

One afternoon, as I'm lifting weights with a couple of young Mexican homeboys, the guards swarm the grass area of the yard, ordering all of the white guys up against the wall. Apparently, too much laughter has convinced them everyone is drunk. While the men on the wall are being searched, a couple of guards are picking up water contain-ers, sniffing for the presence of alcohol. No one is drunk, and there is no booze on the yard. During this period of searching and sniffing, the afternoon in-line is called. I head out of the iron pile toward my building. The whole scene is comical, in a bizarre, prison way. A dozen guys are spread-eagled against a wall and a crew of prison guards is fanning out across the yard hunting for the source of the men's jocularity. My homeboys tell me to be careful; they're after the white boys for a change. Rounding the gate, I look back over my shoulder. A guard is bearing down on me with a determined look on his face. He orders me to get up against the fence. He starts searching me, mumbling something about shit-talking inmates. Put your hands behind your back. Handcuffs are crunched down onto my wrists. The guard starts dragging me off to a facility holding cell. By the time we arrive, the guard has threatened to kick my ass five different ways. He's about half my size. I tell him how impressed I am with his courage while I'm in handcuffs. It's not a pleasant exchange.

Once inside the clinic area, he slams me up against the wall, or rather tries to, with limited success. I'm not about to be smashed into concrete face-first, so I set my feet and lean back against him. Out comes the baton, accompanied by a stream of "Fuck you, assholes," that sort of thing. Just then Sergeant Tyson comes through the door. I was his clerk only a few months before. He may be the only black cowboy I've ever met. At least my height, with a shiny, shaved head and impressively large shoes, he's a rough customer, but fair to a fault. He runs between me and the raving guard, preparing to clock me, and pushes him ranting out the door. An hour later, he returns to report that Mr. V wants me locked up for inciting. I ask him what I incited, but Sergeant Tyson doesn't know. Shortly, all the guys who had been searched on the yard start arriving in handcuffs.

Later, a sheepish Sergeant Tyson and another guard escort me back into medical for a sobriety test and a urine sample. I go through the motions of touching my fingertips to the tip of my nose and standing on one leg without any trouble. A woman medical tech then tells me to walk on a straight line on the floor without looking at it. I guess I fail this test.

She determines I'm drunk. I'm stone-cold sober and have been for a couple of years.

Before the night is over, I'm in a cell in the hole along with the eleven white guys I was supposedly inciting. The next day they're all released from the hole without charge. I receive two serious rules violation reports, one for being under the influence of alcohol and the other for inciting.

The hole at Tehachapi is a different experience from the hole at Soledad, Folsom, or Vacaville. The aggression is out in the open. The guards are primed for combat, and they pride themselves on their well-deserved reputation for kicking ass. To get a shower you have to stand at your cell door wearing only your boxers and shower shoes. If you protest, they pull you out of your cell and leave you locked in the shower for hours without water. If you kick the doors, they drag you out to the exercise yard, chain you to the metal pole of the basketball backboard, and leave you there for the night.

When the results of the urinalysis come back, the under-the-influence charge is dropped. All that remains is the inciting charge. A month into being in the hole, I'm brought to a hearing before Lieutenant Dane, a man I also once worked for, and whom we all generally consider fair. Before I can launch into a defense of myself, he interrupts.

Horse, I know you didn't incite anyone, but I have to find you guilty.

That doesn't seem fair, boss.

I know it's not fair, but I have to do what I'm told to do.

A week later I go to a committee where I'm informed that I've been sentenced to a nine-month security housing unit term. Mr. V is in the room, so pleased with himself that I half expect him to break into a jig. This means I'll be transferred up north to one of the notorious super-max prisons and lose all my property. The level of frustration I feel is intense. I've worked as hard as I could to remake myself and now I'm back in the hole.

That weekend, I'm called out for another non-contact, behind-the-glass visit with Anita. After conjugal visits, after long hours in the visiting room with my gorgeous, wild Mexican girl, glass visits are a serious letdown. Before I make it into the visiting booth, I hear Anita arguing with the guards.

I was told my husband would be out of the hole this weekend, and we would have a contact visit!

We're sorry, Mrs. Hartman, but he's still in the hole.

She goes a couple of rounds with them, then storms into the visiting booth, arguing how the warden promised that I'd be released out of the hole and remain here at Tehachapi. Anita is nothing if not persistent. She wears them down. That week I go back to another committee, where I'm informed that "after a reconsideration that has nothing to do with your wife" they've decided to suspend the security housing unit term and release me to the other max unit down the hill. Mr. V looks a lot less pleased at this committee's verdict. The next day I'm in IV-B, a couple of hundred yards away from IV-A, but an altogether different yard.

California Correctional Institution, Tehachapi: III

IV-B is a much softer, less pressurized place than IV-A. I'm released with Mark Moen, a lanky, six-foot-six, black-haired bundle of issues wound so tight he looks to be about ready to detonate. In the hole he was beaten close to death by the guards and then charged with battery on a peace officer. We both figure we've been celled-up on the assumption that we'll try to kill each other. Instead, we become close friends. I testify in court on his behalf. After hearing four guards in a row testify, in the exact same, scripted words, how Mark attacked all of them in his boxers and shower shoes while handcuffed, the district attorney moves for a recess. When she comes back, she moves to dismiss. The guards are not pleased. We remain cellies until he is paroled a year later.

Mark is the second cellmate I convince to become sober. Both leave my cell to success on parole. We argue all the time, but through them both I refine a militant posture against drugs that will never diminish; if anything, the coming years will only convince me more of how destructive drugs are in the lives of prisoners.

For the first time in years, I don't have a job, nor am I a part of any regular program. I spend my days lifting weights and jogging, trying to reassure the guys on the yard I'm not there to shatter the peace. Anita comes to visit every weekend, as she has for years now. We get back conjugal visits every few months. I'm comfortable in ways I've never been before.

*

One day I notice a posting on the bulletin board for a creative writing class. Anita has told me I should be a writer, an idea that never struck me as more than the puffery of love. I have written a lot of legal briefs in defense of prisoners' rights, but nothing creative. I'm curious to find out if I have any talent, though, so I sign up. The first meeting is in a few weeks, in the afternoon, in the library. In the meantime, I continue to hit the iron pile, wandering around the yard, working to reassure everyone around me that my intentions are good.

The first writing class is interesting mostly because I can't imagine how anything productive can possibly come out of this collection of human odds and ends. The teacher, David Scott Milton, who's working on contract through the sadly underfunded Arts in Corrections program, strikes me as a little too rumpled around the edges himself. The prisoners range from a couple of old cats to a few youngsters, of all hues and sizes, and with a surprising level of literacy. As in a lot of urban high schools, it's not a big social plus to be an intellectual in the joint, and what passes for education in here is limited. Those who have managed to accumulate formal knowledge tend to be autodidacts, and keep it to themselves. David makes a couple of points right off that grab my attention. He teaches in the graduate-level writing program at the University of Southern California and compares us to his exceptionally well-prepared, well-groomed, well-educated students who lack significant life experiences; we have an overabundance of life experiences. Most of us have been run over by life experiences. Next, he compares the process of storytelling to a series of "complications."

He tells us to write three complications by next week. I like assignments.

Unlike most prisoner-writers, I don't fancy myself a budding screenwriter, a songwriter, a poet, or a novelist. I initially see in writing a chance to explore my life, to try to understand all that's happened, to follow the contours of the dark conundrum. I start writing little vignettes of memory, but quickly realize what I must do before I pursue any serious writing. First, and most painfully, I have to apologize for my actions. David suggests I simply write out how I feel about killing Mr. Fellowes. After many false starts, through the process of writing about the trial I discover the one unfortunate commonality he and I shared—neither of us had any family members or loved ones present during the proceedings. We were both alone in the courtroom. Sure, the district attorney claimed to speak for Mr. Fellowes, but he didn't know him. The truth is, I knew Mr. Fellowes better than the D.A. did, and I was the last living soul to speak to him. I was the last human being to hear his gruff voice, to see his face flash with color, to notice his workingman's garb. Before I stole the spark from his eyes, before I killed him, I was the last person he saw on this earth. No one came to the trial on his behalf; no one collected his remains. He simply ceased to exist. All of this caused to well up in me a tremendous sense of guilt and sympathy, a profound connection. He wasn't mourned by anyone. I started off the piece, "Who mourns Thomas Allen Fellowes?"

After I finish reading the much-revised essay in class, there is a moment of silence, followed by a smattering of applause, congratulations, and deep breaths. Without meaning to,

I have broken through the fourth wall of convicted felons, particularly those who have killed. We struggle desperately to remove ourselves, to create distance between the terrible acts we've committed and our hearts. To dig too deeply into any given story is to risk unearthing things we don't want to know. It isn't generally done. David is clearly moved and excited. He asks me what I'm going to do with my essay. I tell him I'll send it to my hometown paper as a kind of public repentance. He thinks it's a great idea so a few days later I mail it to the *Long Beach Press-Telegram*, the same paper that used to land on my family's doorstep every afternoon. The paper my father read every day with the same clockwork regularity that governed everything he did. The paper that brought shame to our common name.

The last time I saw my father was in the county jail a few weeks after I was arrested. He looked bedraggled, wearing an old, green fatigue jacket, a couple of days' growth of silver beard, his brown eyes set a little deeper in the deep creases of his weather-beaten face. On the other side of the thick, dirty glass, I could see the ocean in his face, the longing for rolling swells and calls to battle stations, and exotic, brown-skinned women south of the equator. He'd spent thirty years in the U.S. Navy. He came to get me to sign the pink slip to my piece-of-crap '65 Chevy van so it could be bailed out of impound. There wasn't much to say. He asked if I did it and I lied, because I always lied to him, and told him I didn't. There was no way I could find it in myself to trust my father, though I think I knew even then that he was an eminently trustworthy man. To be honest with my father would have felt like surrender, and I wasn't about to surrender. Then he said, "You know I told you if you went back to jail, that was it." Those were his last words to me, the last words I ever heard him speak. He was greatly offended that the *Long Beach Press-Telegram* had printed our name because his son was arrested for murder. He got up, looked at me one more time, and left.

In addition to telling me to stay away from that goddamned park, he had told me that if I got into any further trouble after I turned eighteen, he would never speak to me again. It may seem harsh now, but it didn't then. He had spent thousands of dollars he didn't have, wasted countless nights hunting for his wayward son, and endured tribulations that only a parent can understand. When a judge pronounced me a ward of the state, no longer under the custody of my parents, my father was in the back of the courtroom. I have always remembered his sad eyes, wet with suppressed emotion. Years later, he brought my brother to some camp for juvenile offenders—a visit neither of us relished. I saw that misty-eyed look again. What's wrong, Dad? It's been a long time since I saw my boys together. By the time he made the final break with me, he must have added up the costs, done the awful calculus, and concluded that he had to devote his resources to my younger brother and sister. I never doubted his resolve. My father was a man of his word. Just as I wouldn't surrender, he wouldn't go back on his word, no matter how much it hurt.

New Folsom

I'm called to R&R to attend the trial regarding the AIDS affair. It has been five years of dueling paperwork, a battle I seem to have won. The state will have to explain why I was lied to, why it informed the entire population I had AIDS, and why the medical system was so shockingly deficient. I'm transported down to the Level III to catch a bus back up to Folsom, to the new joint across a field of time from the granite pit, to appear in the federal courthouse in Sacramento. The bus pulls out of Tehachapi in the early morning darkness under a blank mountain sky. After a day's travel, I'm in a cell in O wing at Soledad (only a tier over from the last one I was in at Soledad), on layover, waiting for another bus farther north. The next morning, back on the road. The guards who drive and man the bus, two in the front compartment, one in the back with a shotgun, exude a hostility that is so disproportionate it has to be an act: There is no talking on the bus! If you think I'm kidding, try me! They wear black jumpsuits and shiny, black combat boots, with their pant legs bloused. We're a rolling, bouncing prison, and they're determined to make sure we're too miserable to allow any glimpses of freedom to intrude on our confinement.

New Folsom, built in 1986, another shouting, pressurized R&R, and I'm taken to the hole. Worse, I'm put in Administrative Segregation/Orientation overflow, a prison version of purgatory. Sort of the hole, sort of orientation, sort of nowhere going slow. I have my four inches of paperwork, a jumpsuit, and a fish kit of toilet paper roll, cheap razor, small plastic comb, and hotel-size bar of soap. New Folsom is the design upgrade from Tehachapi. The same big cells, but with an extra window in the front wall so the visibility is improved—for them. The upper bunk is much higher to make it easier for the guards to run in unimpeded. Several guys break their legs and ankles jumping down before adjusting to the height. The back window is smaller and painted white from the outside so we can't look out. The walls are unpainted cement, which reeks of a damp, earthen musk. The floor is heavily painted to leave a mark if someone grinds a shank. Floor paint is in high demand at New Folsom, a place constructed with the stated intention of preventing violence using the most modern and restrictive means, but which is wildly violent and out of control.

I go to court in another, more ill-fitting jumpsuit, chained in the back of a van with bare metal benches where the seats used to be. In the courtroom, the prison guards assume a posture of barely restrained aggression, constantly shifting from foot to foot, eyeing everyone in the area with open suspicion. I'm thrust into the position of conducting the trial, much like the prosecutor in a criminal proceeding. One of the deputy attorneys general looks over at me and smiles only with his mouth, not his eyes. The judge, a kindly looking black man with a neatly trimmed beard, asks me if I'm ready to start jury selection. I'm so over my head as to be baffled by everything; I'm not sure if directly answering the judge is allowed. The courtroom stalls for a few minutes while everyone waits for the answer. In all my previous appearances in court, I've been a defendant in the position of responding to an allegation, with a lawyer guiding my conduct. I request the appointment of counsel, sensing how ill-prepared and ill-equipped I am. He denies my motion, and goes on about how well I've represented myself in the pleadings. I tell him, Well, let's get started. By the end of the day we've impaneled a six-man jury, with one alternate. I notice that the only remaining deputy attorney general is also a black man. As I'm preparing to leave, I tell the judge this is quite a switch, a white prisoner against a black lawyer in front of a black judge. It seems I'm the only person in the room who appreciates my humor.

The next day I give my opening statement. The problem is, every two sentences the deputy attorney general is objecting. I didn't think you could object during openings. This sets the tone for the trial. I know far too little about civil procedure to compete with someone who does it for a living. My witnesses are all prisoners, except my wife. My guys do the best they can to overcome their shackled walk to the witness stand, surrounded by jumpy guards, but it's a steep climb. Anita, after a withering barrage of objections, comes unglued and storms out of the courtroom yelling, "Liars!" as she slams the beautiful, dark, oak wood doors behind her.

I have managed to compel the attendance of a couple of directors and wardens at the trial. By the time they finish their collective testimony, I would almost believe them, were it not for the fact I was there during the matters in question. It all boils down to a couple of simple questions: Did the defendants subject me to cruel and unusual punishment during my AIDS journey? And did they violate my right to privacy by revealing to anyone who would listen that I had AIDS? My closing argument is so lame as to be a kind of intellectual humiliation. The outcome was never in doubt anyway. After the judge dismisses the case, he feels compelled to give me a long pep talk. Whatever faith I may have held in the judicial system, admittedly not a helluva lot, is emphatically extinguished that day.

During my stay in the overflow unit, I receive a letter from a friend that contains a page from the *Long Beach Press-Telegram*. Under the overwrought headline, "Murderer Is Filled with Remorse for Sin," and accompanied by a drawing that looks disconcertingly like me morphing into a skeleton, my apology fills up half a page of the Sunday opinion section. It is printed verbatim. Though it's a thrill to see my words in print, the subject matter is too disturbing for me to feel good about it. I ultimately receive a number of letters in response to the piece. All of them are positive, ranging from mildly encouraging to downright supportive. The letter I secretly desire, the one from someone in my family, never arrives. I've always wondered what my father thought when he read it.

California Correctional Institution, Tehachapi: IV

It's 1993, and I'm back at Tehachapi on the IV-B yard. My cellie Mark Moen has been paroled from my cell, clean and sober. By this time in my sentence, I've lived with at least a dozen different guys, some better than others, a couple of them horrible and a couple who became great friends. But they're all men, and I'm not gay. When Mark leaves I pay off one of the clerks to keep me in a single cell for a while, the better to assess what I want to do next. The whole revolutionary-leader-fighting-in-the-courts-for-justice trip was a bust. It wasn't simply because I lost in the AIDS trial, though that was surely a part of it. I'm coming to the growing realization that personal transformation is the key to everything I hope to achieve. My public apology was really an appeal to the world to be accepted back into society. The difficulty revolves around my own growth. I feel the need now to dig deeper into my core. Though I've grown considerably over the years, it has been in the direction of how to function from day to day. The reason for my life continues to elude me.

I'm writing regularly, sometimes for days on end. The politics of prison has taken a harsh turn that has rendered me, as a prisoner and as a convicted murderer, a being less than human. Prison has become a much tougher place over the last few years; hard time is even harder now. It hurts. There is a massive disconnect between what I see all around me—people who want to be given a chance—and the prevailing attitude. The oppressive rules and proposed laws assume a lack of possibility, but I know I've changed. The guards have also changed, enforcing procedures that make no sense. I write and publish in newspapers opinion pieces decrying the system. It's all so clear what will happen if the present course isn't altered. Prisoners, like all humans subjected to unreasonable cruelty, will react with violence and irrationality.

Most of the mail I receive is positive. Once in a while, some crazy will write to me, typing so furiously the o's are punched out: You're sick, a piece of shit, you should die for your sins, and so on. But most of my correspondents are more reasonable. Some offer to help me, to send me a package or stamps. The occasional girl wants to start up correspondence for a relationship. One older woman suggests I write a parallel biography of Mr. Fellowes and myself to show our common humanity.

Since those couple of months in the hole at Vacaville, I have maintained an irregular meditation practice. My practice is more disciplined now. Living alone for the first time in years affords me the luxury of setting my own schedule. I sit for hours, escaping this world to a place of calm that overwhelms my perception. Emptiness moves to be filled with a depth of emotion I had forgotten existed. Sitting on the concrete floor of my cell, I search for that essential center from which all will become clear, the mysteries of the universe will unravel before my perfect gaze, the meaning of the words will become known.

While I tussle with my place in the grand scheme of things, Anita is coming to grips with the increasing unlikelihood of my release. The cascade of laws pouring out of the State Legislature has effectively dug a deep moat around the prisons. In the past couple of years there have been attempts to end the conjugal visiting program. Anita has traveled to Sacramento to testify against the bills, but the get-tough crowd's strength is increasing. Her misery is a palpable force that clings to her like a tattered shawl. It doesn't help that I'm disappearing before her liquid, green eyes, so filled with longing and despair. The hours and hours of sitting alone on the floor in meditation have the paradoxical effect of draining me of energy. Each night, I set out on another search, looking for something I cannot name and wouldn't recognize if I bumped into it. Anita thrives on conflict, on passion. She fell in love with and married a red knight, not a contemplative monk. Her desire, her physicality, and her endless battles with everything and everyone wear me out. There are days when I don't speak to anyone. There are long periods when I don't feel connected to the world at all.

I continue to write out of a deep sense of drowning. One of my pieces is published in the *Los Angeles Daily News*, a small regional paper, about the impending "three strikes and you're out" initiative. It's clear to me the law will result in the mass incarceration of wayward dope fiends and young, disaffected gang members under the guise of ridding the world of serial killers and psychopaths. I'm called to the facility office and asked to sign a consent form to be interviewed by the local Fox News affiliate. A few days later, I'm sitting in the boardroom where committee hearings are held with a microphone being attached to my shirt under the glare of hot lights. It turns out a producer read my piece and wants to hear what I have to say, in person, about "three strikes." There's no doubt it will pass into law. I decide to point out what I believe will happen when it does. When the interview airs, I'm acclaimed as a hero amongst my peers, and deemed an enemy of the system by the administration. I enjoy the positive attention.

David Milton, still teaching his writing class and asking for three complications, has become a good friend and mentor.

He encourages me to write an autobiography. I switch jobs to work the graveyard shift, from ten at night until six in the morning, called first watch. It's an odd job for a prisoner, to be out of my cell at hours few of us ever see. I work in the clerk's office, a modified holding cell with a toilet and sink, a radio, a hot pot, and several desks crowded with official forms and battered office typewriters. I am alone for the entire shift. My responsibilities are light. Five nights a week, I type up the masters for the Daily Movement Sheet, a record of all transfers in, transfers out, cell moves, and job changes. I usually get to work about quarter to ten, under a loose escort by the departing swing-shift guards. I plug in the hot pot for coffee, arrange my papers, and turn on the radio to some classic rock. The goal at this point is to trick my body into a state of wakefulness. For years now, I've become a classic early-to-bed, early-to-rise person. One of the graveyard guards brings the pile of papers and the mimeograph masters at around ten thirty. For some reason, they regard the blank masters as hot items, never mind that we have zero access to a mimeograph machine. I do the painstaking typing—no mistakes allowed—and send the completed masters up to control before midnight. Other than stapling, my job is done. I type up a couple of letters to warm up. Then I pull out the manuscript.

It's typed on legal-length paper, single-spaced and double-sided. The text is a deluge of words flooding the empty whiteness, crowding the margins as if to spill over the edges. I start with my first memory, the coughing-into-a-pillow affair, and proceed to pour out every single thing I can recall. It goes on night after night, for weeks, months, this unburdening of memory. I discover many things about myself during this process, not all of them pleasant. For most of my life I have been a selfish and incredibly self-centered person, trapped in a solipsistic reality that allowed me to justify all my transgressions because I felt transgressed against. I was a pathological liar. On those occasions when people tried to help me, I had run full steam in the other direction, headlong back into the comfortable fog of my self-imposed misery. There are moments in the writing when I have to step back and wipe away the tears that cloud my eyes.

It is during this process that I finally come to some understanding of my parents, or at least arrive at a place of empathy and humility. All the years of blame and rage come undone as the life I lived comes back to me. I don't lie to myself, and I can no longer ignore the terrible losses they endured. Small snippets of conversations come back to me. My father's memory of going down to the local tavern in Buffalo, New York, to get a bucket of beer for his father, and his description of how hard it was to make it back without too much spilling. This was before he was orphaned, before his parents were both killed in a car crash, before he was adopted by a widowed German woman named Annamarie in Erie, Pennsylvania. He didn't reveal to me that he was adopted until I was eighteen and claimed German heritage to explain my first swastika tattoos. "I'm not German. Our name is German. I was adopted," he said with the dull finality of a slamming door. But he still remembered being a little boy struggling to please his father. How heavy had that burden been to carry, especially when there'd been no one to share it?

Late one night, my mother told me how her mother had died in the Cocoanut Grove fire. It was just the two of us talking. The mad demon that usually drove her had gone to sleep and the intelligent woman she was deeper down came out. She had been forced to identify her mother's body. She would have been about eleven years old. It still haunted her. I could feel her sadness, its gravity still apparent after thirty years. She described how her otherwise absent father came to collect her from her grandmother, but was rebuffed because he'd abandoned the family. I think my mother's one shot at happiness drove out the driveway of that three-story walk-up on Edson Street in South Boston that day.

In both of my parents, the sadness of their childhood losses colored them a shade grayer. My father always seemed to be removed from the goings-on of daily life, as if he existed across a deep chasm of emptiness. Even so, he had many positive aspects. For a man who had grown up poor, who remembered serious deprivation, who turned off lights in unused rooms and believed that every pair of pants had several lives, he could be as generous as anyone I've ever known. Every Christmas morning, the living room would be piled high with gifts. He couldn't see the sense of wrapping presents, but he truly understood how much kids love that wondrous rush of excitement that a mass of brightly colored toys elicits. On Christmas Eve, we would be banished to our bedrooms until 0600 hours. We would burst out the moment the clock struck. Dad sat in the dining room, a little way back from the commotion, smoking his Lucky Strikes, drinking a cup of black coffee out of a white cup.

My mother, too, for all her wild swings of fury and depression, had much good in her. She was intellectually curious. A tremendous conversationalist, she could hold her own with anyone she met. Out of the house, when the baggy housedresses were retired to the closet and she wore her huge, amethyst ring, her luxuriant black hair piled up over her truly beautiful face, people were always impressed. Tall and commanding, she retained a bit of the grace and strength of the athlete she had been. Like all good South Boston Irish, she idolized and worshipped the Celtics and lamented the hapless Red Sox. I met Ted Williams, she would say with a suggestive inference in her voice. Having seen a black-and-white photo of my mother when she was seventeen, in a one-piece bathing suit, I didn't find it hard to imagine her attracting any man.

When Kay Vanzant, the coolest girl in   Alexander Hamilton Junior High School, pierced my ear and it became infected, my mother acted just as outraged as my father. A few days later, walking through JC Penney, we ended up at the jewelry counter. Pick out a couple of earrings but don't tell your father, she told me, stretching the R out in father until it lost all sense of the letter and became a vowel. When she found out I was smoking, she asked what brand. A carton of Camel regulars habitually turned up in my sock drawer. One time, while I was still at Folsom, I sent a letter addressed to her with a typed label and no return address on the envelope. A couple of weeks later, I got a letter from her in the wild scrawl that fit her so well. She lamented that our second German shepherd, Schultzie, had died. She would never get another dog, it was too painful, she wrote. She didn't answer any of my other letters because of my father's edict. I never heard from her again.

Writing about my parents in the dead of night in a concrete holding cell, I realize how much I have become my father. I have become responsible and serious, and I seek to be respected on account of what I do. It is a complicated thing, this becoming Kenneth Earl. To my knowledge, my father never did anything worse than get divorced from his first wife, and I only know that because I found his personal papers a long time ago, while rummaging around in his closet. In the Navy, he was highly regarded, a leader of men. During the big war, he was a genuine hero who swam from one sinking ship to another, and helped to shoot down a Japanese torpedo bomber coming to finish the job. More to the point, he had guts. He went to night school after he retired from the service to get his high school diploma, and later went to community college. Not a man prone to excited outbursts, he concealed a capacity for intense feeling; I recall him listening to an album of classical music and excitedly describing to me the flowing river of sound in the composition.

I also come to the startling realization that somehow, from deep inside Mother California's barren womb, crushed under the weight of a life without parole, I had managed to find a woman not altogether unlike Patricia Agnes. The same irrationality, the same maelstrom of emotions, the same wounded kindness. Even the dark hair and green eyes, the beauty and intelligence, the strangulated Catholicism and foul mouth . . . somehow I found her. I have done what many men do: I have married a woman much like my mother.

I write, or rather I type, six hundred pages of raw, unfocused words and memories scrunched onto long pieces of paper. Unsure what to do with this outpouring, I give it to David Milton to read. As with everything else I've written, before or since, I feel no ego attachment to it. David brings it back to me a week later and says, "You were a crazy son of a bitch, Ken." He advises me to begin the process of rewriting. He tells me there is a great story in the mountain of words, but I need to find a consistent theme, a reason to read it. I take the pile of paper back to my cell, put it in a box, and slide it under my bed.

Anita has decided that she must have a baby. I'm not in favor of this idea at all. The truth is I'm not sure she is up to the task of being a single mother, and that is the reality she would be facing. Over the past several years, it has become clearer to me how much she remains in denial about the true nature of my sentence. She's not alone in this unwillingness to see life without the possibility of parole as another form of the death penalty. We prisoners, and the officials of the prison system, rarely use the full name, calling it life without parole, or LWOP. Dropping "the possibility of" out of it somehow seems to leave in a little hope. The first time Anita heard it, she assumed it meant when I got out I would not be on parole. Over the years the sentence mutated from a harsher life sentence to a more palatable death sentence. Regardless, the reality is no one who is doing life without parole ever gets out, not in California.

But this is one big turd to come to terms with, and I'm still learning how to do it. Anita remains locked in a fairy-tale ending where the system decides to disgorge me one day, of its own accord I suppose. The truth is, the '90s have changed the direction of prison "reform" so fundamentally that we're all under the assault of the "get tough on crime" era, which really means get tough on prisoners, the captured troops of the enemy forces in the broader War on Crime. By the time Anita has decided she must have a baby, it is finally getting through to me, at least, that I will never get out. The real deal breaker is the impending loss of conjugal visitation, and the approach of my wife's thirty-fifth birthday. For the past couple of years, she has made the trip to Sacramento, the state capital, to testify at hearings on bills to deny all lifers conjugal visitation. She is something of a star at these hearings—a beautiful, articulate, passionate woman possessed of a powerful core message about redemption and humanity. But those arguing for the termination of conjugal visits are unsparing in their visceral disdain for the wives of murderers. Though our side wins every hearing, it is clear that all the abuse takes a lot out of her. Defending sex for killers is a losing proposition.

Besides all the obvious downsides to fathering a child while doing life—not being able to help financially, not being able to contribute physically at all after conception—I'm particularly troubled by two things. The selfish concern revolves around what I have seen all my life inside, the terrible pain of separation that the vast majority of men undergo. Very few prison relationships last beyond a few years, and with the end of conjugal visits in sight, I fully expect the long-term ones to become still more rare. I have seen the hardest men alive demolished by the loss of contact with their children. Be it on account of the fact of imprisonment, the dissolution of a relationship with the mother, or the children not desiring to see the father inside, the result is the same. Right around this time, I watch an older guy, J.P., as tough as they come, disintegrate into a blubbering mass on seeing his four grown children for the first time in twenty years. I'm terrified of this uncontrollable pain.

The less selfish concern is for this child I would be inviting into my life. Through all these years of visiting Anita, I have come to know several children who visit their fathers in prison. There is a heartbreaking quality, a profound sadness about them. A central figure in each of their lives is denied them at the most basic level. I wonder how I would ever answer the inevitable question: What the hell were you thinking? This dilemma has compelled me to deny Anita's entreaties for several years now.

On the other side of the argument is my poor wife, so certain she can handle being a mother by herself, so determined to sway me to her side, so terrified her chance is about to be taken away from her. This is a woman who has literally been with one man in her life—never a drunken mistake, never a fling, never a slip all these years. A woman of uncommon and indisputable virtue. During a conjugal visit, while she is still taking the pill, we discuss the issue deep into the night. Her argument is good, and I am so deeply in love it's difficult to deny her anything. I extract two promises out of her, sealed with a formal handshake: We will do everything possible to give any child we create a better life than either of us had;

no beatings, no cold withdrawal of emotions or denial of the fundamental rights of this innocent being we seek to call out of the void. And no matter what happens between us—if we fall out of love, if the stress of being married to a man likely to grow old and die in prison simply becomes too much—this child will never be kept from his or her father, hard as that promise may be to live up to. It's strange how, like all people who haven't had children of their own, we are so wholly and completely unprepared for what we are about to do. Of course, at some level, I question the odds of pregnancy. We are both in our mid-thirties. We can have sex only every couple of months for two days, which are out of our control to choose.

I am tired of writing editorials, tired of shouting out into the real world about how bad things are getting inside the joint. More and more, I spend my time exercising, reading magazines, and studying academic textbooks. This is one of the periods in my life when I need to lie fallow, to deepen what I know and create new connections, develop a broader grasp of reality. With Anita's help—she is now the legal secretary to one of the chief counsels to Bank of America, and earning a nice wage—I gather together piles of books related to criminology, penology, and the many variants between the two, along with a collection of prisoner's rights newsletters. My goal is to try to figure out my world. Everything is changing so rapidly. What was okay yesterday is now illegal. The programs that took decades to pull together are collapsing, burning down in the incendiary rhetoric of California's political firestorm. State legislators are proposing laws so bizarre it's hard to take them seriously. Chain gangs; vast, enclosed tent camps in the low desert; forcing prisoners to pay for medical care; closing all educational programs, all job training, and moving all lifers without parole to Alaska . . . The upshot is to send a clear message to the guards that they can take off their gloves and get seriously rough. This is not something they need to be told twice.

The "three strikes and you're out" ballot initiative wins by a large margin. There's no doubt what is coming—a tidal wave of angry gangbangers and pathetic drug addicts sentenced to life. I remember how I was one of the early '80s wave that swamped Folsom. Now, more than a dozen years later, it's my boat getting rocked, and I don't like it a bit. I want to enjoy my visits and packages. I want to experience what continuity and stability there is to be had. I have transformed myself into someone I couldn't have imagined only a decade earlier. I have read a small library of books. I have been to a couple of hundred hours of group therapy and twelve-step meetings. I have gotten my writing published in a bunch of newspapers and a few magazines. I've been interviewed on television and quoted on the radio. I have the hottest old lady in the visiting room, and the sex is so good it defies description. Anita is lithe and willing and enthusiastic like no woman I have ever known. She has an orgasm while French kissing, and she's willing to do anything to please. Her own pleasure is so intense that her screams can be heard on the yard.

I'm in love, and being in love has radically changed me. It has made me willing to take the chances I've taken. The small chances, like really participating in therapy, in all those irritating twelve-step meetings. I wouldn't have stopped getting high but for the fear of losing love. I wouldn't have cracked the covers of law books and textbooks if I had continued to get stoned. None of these things could ever have happened if I had remained locked in the loveless grasp of Mother California.

Then there are the big chances I took on account of this experience of love. After a couple of years at Tehachapi, when the prison system finally rounded up the fellas and poured them into the bottomless pit of the indeterminate-sentence lockup program, when it became clear there was no easy way back through that labyrinth to rule the asphalt yards, I started to receive kites from some of them. At first they were little, coded messages of greeting. What's shaking brother? How you doing stud? Pretty soon the tone became harsher, more insistent, as the yards started to fill up with enemies of the fellas. Lists of names came, those in the hat, marked for attack. I suppose they figured I would either off those names myself or assign someone to the task. I flushed the kites and lists down the toilet. After a while there were no more kites.

The biggest chance I took because of love was to look into myself. For my whole life I had fought to free myself of sentiment, to steel myself against emotion. This effort left me thrashing about and sore, always ready to lash out, to surrender only to negative emotion. "We are not thinking beings who feel, we are feeling beings who think." I can't remember where I read this, but it made so much sense to me that I had it written out in calligraphy and hung it on my cell wall. There's no way to stop feeling, just as there's no way to stop breathing. There are ways to stop thinking, as I learned early in life. Drugs don't kill off feeling, they only dull the ability to analyze and assess emotion. Through all those years when I was hiding from how I felt, the struggle seemed to be about suppressing the pain of my life, self-inflicted though much of it was. I felt as if I had been doing math with a broken calculator, one that always gave the wrong answer. The harsh truth of it is, I felt stupid.

*

Anita tells me we need to have a conjugal visit at exactly the right time to conceive. These visits are scheduled by a guard who turns out to be surprisingly supportive. He tells me that Anita and I are viewed as the perfect couple; everyone can see how much we really love each other. She does the calculations and comes up with the ideal weekend. I get it locked in, but a few weeks after she gives me the first set of coordinates she comes up with a different set of desirable dates. We are rescheduled to these new dates. Of course, when the day arrives and we are in the apartment together, she tells me the first set of coordinates was the right set, after all. It's too late to change. Two weeks later, during a regular visit, she announces that she's pregnant.

This is not the first time I've heard this news. Anita is more than a touch hypochondriacal. Like my mother, as hard as it is for her to hear every time I point it out, she tends to imagine all kinds of ailments and bodily troubles. In the seven years we've been enjoying conjugal visits, she has imagined she was pregnant about half the times we've together. For every visit, she's been on the pill, and the one time she wasn't I used condoms. This was also the first time I saw how easily she could come unglued. After a couple of times together, I found out how little I enjoyed the act with a condom. "If you get pregnant, you could just get an abortion." *I* still came first.

She was sitting across from me on the floor, her clothes in a pile to her side, pulling on a pair of black cowboy boots. Anita's head popped up, her green eyes ablaze "Don't ever ask me to kill my baby!" She shouted as one of the boots came flying at my head, missing me by inches. It took me hours to talk her down from the heights of her fury.

Before coming to the last conjugal visit, she takes an HIV test, just to be sure. After another week, she has seen a doctor. She really is pregnant. I marvel at both her fertility and her shift in personality. Anita is transformed.

I am not transformed. Nothing seems to have changed, certainly not outwardly. Visits still happen almost every weekend. I still go to work in the miserable Prison Industry Authority's chair factory. My time as a late-night clerk ended when some lieutenant concluded that lifers without parole couldn't work at night. After a string of published stories, I was sent a disciplinary infraction notice for conducting a business in my cell. I could have challenged it and easily won, but I had lost the zest for writing about the prison system. Besides, I was making too many enemies. The guards take criticism very personally and my fellow prisoners see any commentary from this world as tantamount to revealing state secrets.

I work out every day, running a few miles and hitting the iron pile, with a second workout every third evening. I do a fairly thorough yoga routine followed by meditation. I gave up television a couple of years ago, along with a mattress; I sleep on the bare metal of my rack on top of a blanket. I have come to the conclusion I must voluntarily deny myself to achieve some higher level of consciousness. (In retrospect, I think all I got out of it was a sense of moral superiority.) Most of my free time I spend reading, or writing letters on my little Canon electronic typewriter.

I write to my long-time friend Linda and ask her to come up to visit. Back in 1988, when she was engaged to marry one of Anita's numerous brothers, she found out the dark family secret, the brother-in-law in the joint. Being an adventurous sort, she wanted to meet me. Although the engagement fell apart, in the ensuing years we've become very close. The joke around the visiting room is that I have a hot Mexican wife and a hot blond girlfriend; I never discourage these rumors. I ask Linda to be my stand-in for the pregnancy process, the classes and appointments, and for the main event itself. She agrees. Beyond this, I'm disconnected from the pregnancy. All I know is two things: One is that I would rather have a daughter because I fear what my incarceration would do to a boy more. The other is that the future, always uncertain for a prison relationship, is more uncertain than ever. If being a couple was stressful, what will it be like to be a family?

But Anita continues to transform and to amaze me. She becomes calmer; she laughs more easily; she softens at every edge, literal and metaphorical. A pretty woman as long as I've known her, Anita has always been a bit too concerned about being thin. After every conjugal visit, I'm bruised; two days of banging into her pelvic bones is an exquisite torture. Now, she rounds out. Her hips spread just enough to be comfortable instead of tight. The skin on her face is softer. Maybe it's a trick of nature, but being with child she has never been so attractive. I'm so crazy in love with her that the last broken parts of me are reconnecting.

Still more surprising, she seems to smooth out inside, too. Her complaints and fears and unquenchable needs lose some of their toxic ferocity. We discuss this impending revolution in our lives in measured tones. Child care, living arrangements, possible career opportunities, all the normal conversations I would imagine expecting couples have on the other side of the electric fences. The most astonishing part of this, beyond even the enhanced beauty of my already beautiful wife, or her new rational manner, is the way it's taken me out of prison. Somehow, after all these years, after all the wrong I've done, a part of me has managed to make it back out to the real world. This strikes me as a sort of miracle.

The chair factory where I work is a hell of sawdust and noise. Since the decision came down that lifers without parole can no longer work at night, and given my published criticism of the prison system, I'm not welcome in the clerk realm. We make office chairs for other governmental agencies in California. Somewhere in the more enlightened past, a law was passed that made it mandatory for all state agencies to buy what we prisoners make. At Folsom it was the old standby, license plates, or "tags" as we called them. At Soledad it was underwear, jeans at Tehachapi and chairs here at IV-B. Prison Industry Authority jobs are generally the most sought after because of the relatively high pay, which starts at thirty-five cents and goes all the way up to ninety-five cents an hour. The downside of this prosperity is that it brings out the worst, most rapacious backstabbing of any jobs in prison. Because I have no interest in making the higher pay grades, or in becoming a master chair maker, I tell the supervisor I don't want a pay raise or a position upgrade. All I want is to be left alone. I spend my six hours a day, five days a week, mostly pushing around pallets of unfinished chair parts from one noisy station to another.

One of the guys I work with is the sweat leader for the Native American spiritual circle. Steve and I spend a good part of the day talking politics and spirituality, a subject I've never felt too comfortable discussing. Ever since leaving home and my mother's brand of regret-filled Catholicism, I haven't thought much about the various brands of organized religion. I am, generally, an atheist during the day and an agnostic at night, when my thoughts turn to the eternal whys and hows. For the past several years, in addition to all the self-improvement books, I've read spiritual works sporadically. But I'm not convinced. I believe in the real, the rational, the demonstrably true.

Steve's faith is both self-assured and non-condescending. It's rooted in the practice of the traditions of indigenous peoples of this hemisphere, and is part of their identity. When I mention that Anita is part Yaqui, a tribe from the Southwest, he tells me about the sweat ceremony and suggests that it would be good for her. By this time, after years of discussion, Anita is pretty much an atheist herself. I know this isn't for her, but I express an interest in participating in a sweat ceremony. One Saturday morning my cell door opens. The guard in the control booth asks me over the loudspeaker if I'm going to the "Indian thing" on the yard. His tone of disapproval helps motivate me to say yes.

It's a cool, spring, mountain morning. I walk up to the gate of the sweat lodge area. Steve is waiting with a shell in which pungent herbs smolder. He waves the smoke over me, a ritual called a "smudge." I'm invited in and directed to a cluster of Native Americans, maybe eight guys, sitting together on the ground. Steve tells me this is the Circle, and I need to speak before I can be allowed to participate in the sweat ceremony. I surprise myself when I profess a sense of longing for a spiritual life, for a connection to something greater; that I have searched for meaning in the rational world, but I still feel incomplete and unfulfilled. I describe those few moments in my life when I felt truly connected to a different kind of reality that eluded me most of the time. I'm honest about my doubts, but I feel drawn to the experience.

One old Apache, Mike, clearly the most resistant to the presence of a white guy on their turf, asks me if I will be respectful of their traditions. I give you my word that when I am on your sacred ground I will be conscious and respectful of what you believe. He sticks his hand out and we shake. He looks me in the eye and slides his hand up to my forearm, mine on his. This is how we do it, brother. With that, all the others clasp my arm the same way. Steve is last. I'll tell you how to prepare for next week. Welcome to the Circle, brother. We will pray for your wife and child. The next Saturday I participate in one of the most intense experiences of my life, and I feel a tremendous sense of the spiritual. Out of allegiance to the tradition I swore to uphold, I can't write about what happened there; I will only say that my life was deepened and opened up in ways I would never have expected. I wept for my wife, for our unborn child, for all peoples, and for all my relations.

The new practical and reasonable Anita has an amniocentesis because of her age. Although we agreed to learn the sex of our child the natural way, she now knows. When she tells me, she is tentative but reassuring: I know all fathers want a son, but they come to love their daughters, too. She doesn't know me as well as she thinks. I have long concluded that I desire a daughter, perhaps because of all the little girls over the years in prison visiting rooms who seem drawn to me. Whatever the reason, I'm extremely pleased.

I want to name her Katherine Elizabeth so we'll have the same initials. It's selfish, I know, but not *that* selfish; I desire every chance to build connections. Anita nixes this: the name is too Anglo. I sense she would rather be connected to the baby's name herself, so I compile a list of names beginning with the letter A. Shortly thereafter, during a visit, she casually refers to the life inside her as "Alia." I take it her name is Alia? That's what I've been calling her. Alia Marie, I tell Anita, and we settle on that full name. It only dawns on me later how close that is to Annamarie, the name, I'm fairly certain, of the German woman who adopted my orphaned father. (I surmise this because of the time, when the subject of children came up, that he requested I name a daughter Annamarie. He said the name so wistfully it obviously held some deep significance.)

Anita finally starts to show, the growing bulge an object of fascination to my fellow prisoners. I share the progress of this incredible event with everyone I meet. Once, after I pass around a print of an ultrasound of little Alia to a group of guys, a guard pulls me off to the side. He tells me I shouldn't talk to other prisoners about Anita's pregnancy, it'll just make them unhappy about what they've lost. I respond, You really don't know prisoners. And he doesn't. The appearance of this child in our midst has a truly magical effect. Out in the visiting room, guys I barely know ask me if I would let them feel the growing expanse of my wife's abdomen. I always say yes, and Anita doesn't seem to mind. I think she understands this child is a part of all of us. Creating life isn't a possibility for most of the men. This incipient being was created right on the grounds of this prison, just fifty yards back from the buildings, out behind the main kitchen. The only ones made uncomfortable are the guards. It simply doesn't square with the system; a pregnant wife, her radiance, the force of new life an aura around her, is too normal, too human.

*

Small things change, often detected only in retrospect; cumulatively they add up to a sea change. When I first came to prison, every Christmas the cell blocks were decorated with lights and wreaths and green trees. Many of us decorated our cells, commonly with the cards we received in the mail. Every meal was a celebration of the holiday. They served us Christmas-tree cookies with green and red sprinkles. In the visiting room, one of the old guys dressed up as Santa Claus for pictures with the kids and the young wives. On Christmas Eve, every prisoner received a shopping bag filled with goodies. Every year, we got a new comb and an address book from the Salvation Army, a few pieces of fruit, a bag of mixed nuts, and a bag of holiday-themed hard candy. Sometimes there would be a couple of cans of soda, maybe a new pen and some writing paper. It was Christmas, even for us.

By the time my daughter is about to be born, fifteen years later, it's December 1995—deep into the get-tough era. There is no Santa in our visiting room, nor are there any decorations. The walls are the same unadorned concrete every day of the year. My first Christmas at Tehachapi, one of the guards got on the public address system to tell us about the great meal he would soon be enjoying, the time he would be spending with his family. We didn't deserve to be with our families, he ranted, we were just where we belonged and have a hearty Merry fucking Christmas. The goody bag days are long since over; our present now is a small bag of unsalted nuts and a bag of broken candy. The holidays have been banished from prison. Little do we know how much worse it will get.

Anita drives up through the mountains on Christmas Day to see me. She always comes for the holidays. It makes her sad to imagine me alone. She is seriously big, her stomach stretched beyond imagining. There have been no complications during the past eight and a half months. She worked right up to the week before the holidays. I'm so completely impressed by my wife; she is a soldier. The older women in the visiting room tell her it is time to let the baby come.

It seems that older mothers, on their first child, tend to hold the process up longer than is necessary. She's due the middle of January, but the general consensus is "that baby is plenty big enough now." We have a good day. I feel Alia moving around. How utterly incomprehensible it is to me. No matter how hard I try, I simply can't imagine what it must be like to have another being alive inside you. On our last conjugal visit, late in October, I laid my ear on Anita's bulge and listened. Nothing at first, but I talked softly to the child I didn't yet know. Suddenly, I heard a distinct scratching sound, as if she were trying to reach out and touch me. I encourage Anita to start preparing herself to let the baby out.

These past months I've forgotten I'm living in prison. I'm part of a project that is all out there, out in the real world, down in the San Fernando Valley, that Kansas of houses and strip malls stretching away in every direction. At least twenty times I have ventured into the inky blackness of the sweat lodge, traveling to places I didn't know existed. All the years of working to overcome my own limitations, struggling to transcend the constraints of my reality, had borne fruit, literally. There is now this profound connection between me and everyone else. From the loud and aggressive man I created, a force that parted the waters of crowded humanity around me with menace and fear, has emerged a still loud and only slightly less aggressive man—but one reaching through barriers to seek connection. I am now a toucher. I touch the people I talk to; I throw my arms around everyone. In my speeches during twelve-step sessions, I adopt one of the program mantras—"You cannot think your way to better living; you have to live your way to better thinking"—as my personal credo. I'm not, after all, a man of books, though I've read a lot of them; I'm a man of action. The racist burden I helped to perpetuate cannot be undone by reforming my thinking. I make it a point to touch black people, to throw my arm over their shoulders, to physically break the barriers that divide us so effectively. I do it in the same determined way I used to pursue my quest to be somebody in the joint. My worst trait, my irrational stubbornness, I redirect toward the good.

I am watched, just as I used to watch the fellas, and knowing this I know it is possible to affect those around me. In prison, so much of what happens is part of a show—a mad, violent circus in which we are the dancing bears, the trapeze artists, the clowns. Under the big tent of this brutally unnatural environment, few of us ever take the frightening step of analyzing our deeper motives. As a younger man, I aspired to be one of the legends of the prison world. To be talked about in hushed tones, with fearful reverence, this was my goal. The trouble was I only had one way to achieve this, a destructive and self-immolating one. Now, I have another foundation on which to build a worthwhile life: the role of reformer, of healer, takes clearer shape.

*

I'm awakened by the first watch sergeant at 3:00 a.m. on the day after Christmas. Mama's in the hospital, he tells me in his folksy, Bakersfield accent. Everything is fine. He gives me a phone number to call later that day. As soon as the phones are available, the guards put me on. I talk to one of my brothers-in-law and my mother-in-law. Anita is in labor. My loyal and lovely friend Linda is with her. Later, I learn Anita had left the visiting room, gone back to her apartment, and told the baby she was ready before going to sleep. She had woken up a few hours later in labor. She refused any pain medication and struggled through twelve hours of agony that ended with forceps pulling my big daughter out. All in attendance told me how brave Anita was, how composed and focused. I'm not surprised. When we finally talk, she sounds exhausted but triumphant. I have never experienced such an intense and overwhelming love than at that moment, nor have I felt more determined to exceed myself.

Two weeks later, I'm on my way out to the visiting room, walking across the sterile yard that still looks unfinished ten years later. The concrete walls have never been painted. What grass there is consists of clumps, and the areas that were dirt then are still dirt now. After more than a decade of operations, there is still no sign on the door to the visiting room. It's simply another steel-and-Plexiglas door.

I enter the visiting processing area, turn in my identification card, and submit to a search before walking into the room. Anita and Linda are both there, along with an impossibly tiny bundle of pink blanket. Linda is very protective of Anita, as if she's just returned from a battle at sea and doesn't quite have her land legs back. Anita steps toward me. Here is your daughter. I'm in a closed space, a silent, white room, just the three of us. When I take the baby into my hands, I marvel at how little she is, how insubstantial and light. My hands are bigger than all of her. Hello Alia.

One of my closest friends, Steve Agin, who has since passed on to greater judgment, was paroled from my cell. A frequent loser, he had grown up a child of Mother California. Like all of us who master this universe, he paid for the lessons with a large measure of his humanity. Unlike me, he didn't have a long-term love affair to temper the ill effects. After he was paroled, he married a woman he met while she was still a prison guard. They had a son. Shortly after this surprising turn of events, I received a letter from Steve. He was exceptionally well-read, and his letters were always full of sly observation and unexpected insights. This letter's tenor was wholly different, more simple and direct as he wrote, "I can't explain it, brother, but when I held my son something inside of me changed. It is as if there is a bell inside that only your children can ring."

Holding my daughter, I hear the bell inside me peal. My eyes are flooded with real tears. The feeling is primal and ethereal, a gathering of hairy ape-men dancing around a fire, watching the orange sparks twirl up into the cold night air. Right there, wrapped in the quiet, contented ball I hold in my hands, I know I have escaped the bonds of prison. It is a relief to grasp this so completely. What is left of me inside the electric fences can concentrate on living this life, such as it is, and give up the longing for release that crouches in the back of all our minds. Somehow, I also sense a shift in the great scales. I took a life, without justification or reason; I stole the light from Mr. Fellowes. Now I have added light to the interconnected web. This doesn't absolve me of guilt, or release me from my obligation to atone for my actions. But as I stand there holding in my arms the being I called into existence, I know I have become a contributor, a participant. I have committed the most human of acts, procreation. I am fully a human being, and I have proof.

*

It is another time of great change in the prison system. The past decade of takeaways has created an increasingly hardened class of prisoners. To combat this growing menace, the system has decided to separate the maximum-security joints into a more dangerous group called 180s on account of the buildings' floor plans, and a less dangerous group called 270s. (The numbers indicate the field of vision available to the gunner in the central booths; the lower number means he needs to cover a smaller area.) The violence has gotten out of hand. Riots are breaking out. Guards are being attacked. The solution is obviously to turn the screws tighter: this is the only way the prison commanders know. The associate warden who reassured me that no one really does life without parole would be surprised by the officials of classification committees nowadays, who remind us, with relish, how we will indeed spend the rest of our lives in prison, till death do us part. In the past fifteen years, the prison population has doubled and then doubled again. One lieutenant I worked for, a pilot in his off time, once told me he could fly from Los Angeles to Sacramento, a good four hundred miles, by following the lights of the prisons in the Central Valley at night. The crackdown of the '90s is in full swing.

I can stay at Tehachapi if I want, but the prospect of greater restriction isn't appealing. Besides, there's the issue of Anita driving up the mountain roads with a new baby. The obvious option is the lone prison in Los Angeles County, a 270-maximum in Lancaster. It will shave an hour off her trip. Although leaving any place you've known for eleven years is unsettling, it isn't hard to leave Tehachapi. Unlike Folsom, this is a prison with no hold on my identity. I've lived in cells here that no other man has served time in before. I've married, made love, conceived a child, but I've never felt rooted to the bland, smooth concrete buildings. Even though the mountains rise around the yard and forests are in view, this prison has a featurelessness that sets it apart from the environment. The real world ends definitively at the demarcation line ten yards on the other side of the fences where "no man's land" begins. Inside this circle of towering chain link wrapped at the top by a coil of razor wire, punctuated by a menacing, armed obelisk every hundred yards, exists a place out of time. Leaving here will be like leaving nowhere.

I remember the first week after I arrived from Folsom. One of the top administrators came down into the dayroom. We were transferred in before the yard was finished so we were restricted to the little side yards adjoining the buildings, tiny enclosures with twenty feet of naked concrete walls. Everyone was feeling the pent-up frustration of being boxed in. The administrator started off by telling us of their plans for the facility—good jobs, vocational training, college, drug counseling. This will be a model institution, he told us. A decade later, after all the shootings, the restrictions on everything from food to exercise to visiting, and the many outrageous abuses, his words leave a bitter taste. I am tired of this place.

The day I leave Facility IV-B for Lancaster, I have no lingering sense of loss or regret. Nor do I have any dope shoved inside of me, or plans to spread mayhem. All I bring with me, besides my allotted six cubic feet of property, is a growing awareness of the need for a greater dimension to my life, a more significant rationale than a couple of more reps on the iron pile, or another article written. What I don't have is any feasible outlet for this desire. As the bus pulls away, I don't look back.

California State Prison, Los Angeles County: Part I

The noise is overwhelming, a constant, throbbing, angry cacophony that pours into my cell all day and most of the night. It's as if the volume knob of the building is stuck at ten and no one knows how to turn it down. Partly, it's the fault of the physical design, which is set up for the perceived needs of the guards and without any apparent consideration for the two hundred men packed inside. Instead of a solid door, there is a metal screen with hundreds of half-inch holes drilled through. The cell is smaller than Tehachapi's, but larger than Folsom's—six feet wide by ten feet deep with two metal racks, two six-cubic-foot metal lockers, a stainless steel toilet-and-sink combo, and a metal desk and stool affixed to the back wall. There is a large light fixture on the ceiling, with a night-light that's always on. A four-inch slit of a window runs from about halfway up the back wall almost to the ceiling, right above the desk.

The building itself is a large, angular U shape of two tiers, fifty cells on the upper tier and fifty on the lower. In the center of the open space between the arms of the U is the control booth, which sits on top of a ten-foot sally port leading out to the yard. The inside end of this sally port is a large grill gate, and the outside end is a solid metal door. From the ceiling, thirty feet up, hang a couple of dozen yellowish lights and yards of dirty, exposed ductwork. This is the new, standard, tilt-up-construction prison building. At this place, there are five of these buildings on each of four facilities: four thousand maximum-security prisoners. (There is also a minimum facility outside the electric fences.) When the California State Prison of Los Angeles County, down in the bowl of a prehistoric lake bed sandblasted by the dreaded Santa Ana winds, opened in 1993, it was under the pretense of a calculated fiction. These cells are the minimum recommended size for one person. The entire infrastructure assumed one man per cell. Of course, two racks were welded in before a single prisoner even set foot in any cell.

Two hundred men in a building designed for half as many and four thousand in a prison designed for two thousand means the level of tension is not merely doubled, but it is an entire order of magnitude greater, following basic laws of human nature. It also means the guards are overwhelmed. Here, the response has been abdication. In a sense, it is a return to the Folsom policy of willful neglect. After a decade of hyper-aggressive micromanaging at Tehachapi, the unruly nature of Lancaster is unsettling in the extreme. The guards here seem to spend most of their time locked inside the building office, standing in little groups at the corners of the yard, or else they're simply not around. Now and again, I look out across the yard and can't find a single guard in sight. Even the control tower often appears unmanned, but this is impossible.

The effect of this surrender of authority is bedlam. A constant stream of guys pours in and out of the housing units. The chapel is a forum for hand-to-hand combat and a crack house. The amount of drugs in circulation is simply astounding. The heavy, sweet pungency of marijuana fills the air. The fruity stench of pruno—prison-made alcohol—is everywhere. Dope is so prevalent I can often smell the chemical dirt odor of tar heroin. Almost everyone is either drunk or high, with all the attendant ills of that lifestyle. Before I'm off fish row, I have been offered every kind of drug imaginable. At the same time, guys from the main line have tried to bum instant coffee off of me. One of the effects of the prolific drug trade is the utter impoverishment of the yard. Most of the users live in empty cells, having sold off all of their worldly goods for the last fix. Meanwhile, a tiny minority of the well connected are living extremely comfortably, their cells packed to the brim with all manner of candies and canned foods.

After the aggressive guards at Tehachapi, I have grown used to a relatively peaceful and orderly life. This is not going to be possible at Lancaster. On account of my age, I am assigned to the most functioning yard, but even here there is a fundamental level of chaos that is accepted as the norm. (When the supervising counselor asks me how long I've been in the joint, he picks up my central file and weighs it in his hand. You must be programming, he tells me, your file is light.) Boom boxes blare out till the wee hours of the morning. Nothing runs on any kind of schedule. To get to sleep, I am forced to use earplugs every night. If someone had set out to create a dysfunctional prison, this would be it.

I request assignment to a computer technology class. The instructor, a pretty, young woman named Demree, is a competent and clearly sensitive person who is utterly out of place in this madhouse. We quickly bond as she recognizes in me someone striving to grow in an environment opposed to growth of any positive kind. As soon as I start the class, I ask for the curriculum to see what requirements I need to graduate. They still haven't approved a curriculum, she tells me. How long has it been since you requested one? Two years. I push on her to get one as soon as possible. It turns out that no one has finished the class, and there is a tacit assumption that no one will. When I talk with my fellow students, I discover that several have been in the class for a couple of years and made very little progress. Before I ultimately receive my certificate of completion, Demree will have to purchase some of the course-required materials herself.

Concurrent with the computer class, I take an accounting course. The materials for this are in an unwrapped box sitting on a shelf in the education department. It turns out Demree was a controller for a real estate company before embarking on the idealistic journey of becoming a teacher in prison. It is old-fashioned, double-entry accounting done by hand on balance sheets, a lost and obsolete skill now done more quickly and accurately on a computer. I see it as a way to bring order to my thinking while I swim in the disorder all around me. I spend many nights hunched over a pile of accounts receivable notes and checks issued by a fictitious company, earplugs firmly crammed in, penciling tiny figures into tiny boxes. Sometimes it feels like the whole course was designed for tiny hands.

The yard is strictly divided by race, each group manning its territory as if defending its patrimony. There are all kinds of bizarre and inane rules that most of my fellow prisoners regard as nearly sacrosanct. You aren't supposed to walk out of the shower before putting your boots back on. This is, ostensibly, because we all have to be prepared to fight at any time. There are two dayroom areas—the blacks are on one side, the whites and Mexicans uncomfortably share the other. The occupants of one side are never supposed to cross through the other's side; you have to go all the way around the perimeter. Again, this is due to the constant preparations for war. The six different shower stalls are divided up among the groups. The clothes irons are divided up by race. The television on the black side invariably has black shows, the other one Spanish-language programming. (There are so few whites, we rate low on the television schedule.) The telephones are allotted by race. The separation is so complete that it outstrips any official policy of apartheid that a racist government could design. The saddest thing about it is that we have done this to ourselves, adopted these separatist policies as holy writ.

Drugs dominate Lancaster. At other prisons where I have served time, drugs are also an integral part of the life of the joint, but the leadership holds drug addicts in low esteem. Never trust a dope fiend, was one of the first admonitions I had received from the fellas. Although we all used, there was an expectation of self-control, of restraint. Prison is a place of titanic stress levels as we are all pulled and pushed and deformed. Surrendering to the call of drugs reduces the ability to resist this pressure. I saw the impact of this firsthand at Folsom. One of my homeboys took off on an extended crank run that ended with him jamming his head into a locker. He had succumbed to the paranoia of speed in a place where bad things do happen.

The biggest shift in Lancaster is that the leadership, such as it is, consists of committed dope fiends. Among the whites, at least, this means the selfish, self-centered, self-destructive worldview of the drug addict has become the prevailing ethos. There is an echo of Folsom, of the "up north" system, but it's so distorted as to be nearly unrecognizable. In Folsom, the fellas were so popular, so idolized, that they had to turn away the majority of guys who wanted to take part in the show. This new breed of shot-callers is forced to demand obeisance because they are held in such contempt by the majority of the men. They're dope fiends with too many tattoos, and they're in collusion with the guards. The prison system has sunk to such an abysmal low here it is shameful.

Nowhere is the degeneration of this world more apparent than in the visiting room. My first few visits with Anita are a disaster. Like everything else here, it's too small, less than half the size of Tehachapi's but with easily three times the number of visitors. Physically, it's an improvement—instead of the concrete cavern we endured for the past decade, this room has many large windows that look out toward the parking lot. But that's the only improvement. There's a patio that isn't used. The area designed for children to play is cluttered with microwaves. The guards assign seating to the tiny tables that are packed so close to each other it's hard not to overhear conversations. The food available in the vending machines is expensive and crummy—dry hamburgers in plastic wrappers, stale chips, lukewarm soft drinks. On account of the crush of visitors, the machines are usually empty. The room is filthy.

This prison, an anarchic Lord of the Flies institution, runs the most disrespectful and mean-spirited visiting program any one of us has ever seen. I speculate that having lost control of the yards, the guards assuage their shame by picking on our wives and mothers and children. It starts in the processing area, on the other side of the fence. Anita waited an hour at most to be processed in at Tehachapi; here, her wait is never less than three hours. The abuse is intolerable. Guards take turns making up new rules about dress standards—one day a pair of pants is acceptable, the next it is not. More than once, Anita is provoked into an argument and sent away for the day after waiting for hours.

Inside the visiting room, it's just as bad. At Tehachapi, we could all take a stroll around the room; it was a part of the program and a great stress reliever. Here, on my first visit, I'm shocked to see visitors and prisoners glued to their seats and afraid to get up. Afraid, even, to talk to one another. Whenever the room at Tehachapi got too crowded, the guards would ask for voluntary double-ups, meaning two prisoners and their respective visitors sharing a table. We often viewed it as a chance to play couples' card games. Here, simply exchanging a greeting is grounds for terminating a visit. If you protest—even for something as innocent as asking why you're being terminated—you can expect to lose visiting privileges for a month, or more.

Our first visit at Lancaster sets the tone for the upcoming years. Anita battles through hours of processing. She sits in the visiting room for an hour before I finally make it out. (They claim they can't find me. Besides the obvious— how can a man be "missing" inside a maximum-security prison?—I'm, as always when waiting for a visit, in my cell.) She has already been admonished about talking to the other visitors. We kiss and embrace before she starts to unload on me about the indignities she's been through. It's hard to listen to because there's essentially nothing I can do about it. At some point, little Alia starts making hungry noises. Anita throws a blanket over herself and lets Alia nurse. The female guard in charge of the room goes apoplectic, yelling, You can't do that in here! She banishes Anita to the women's bathroom and refuses to allow her a chair. Neither of us thinks this is a fair policy so we decide to appeal it to the warden.

A month or so later, the warden, to his credit, has decided that forcing nursing mothers to stand in a cramped bathroom is not a reasonable policy. He authorizes nursing inside the visiting room. We assume that's that. This, after all, is a military-style, hierarchical system. The warden is the commanding officer. Anita is back in the visiting room, nursing.

The same officer is back, red-faced and yelling. Anita tells her the warden has specifically authorized breast-feeding.

I don't give a fuck what the warden said. He don't run this room, I do. Your visit is terminated.

I tell Anita to just go, don't react. Once she leaves the female officer says she ran Anita off because nobody goes over her head. I tell her Anita and I will still be visiting and she won't be working out here. Before this particular battle is over, Anita and I will file multiple appeals, and more than one supervisor will be reassigned.

Dealing with the needs of Anita and Alia is a complicated balancing act. Alia is so irresistible that Anita recedes into the background of my attention. It's the all-in rush of new love, when you can't get enough. Early on, it's obvious that Alia doesn't want to be separated from me—she literally doesn't want to be out of physical contact for one minute during the course of a visit. My joy is tempered by guilt: What will happen to her? What the hell were you thinking?

Even though I know I am neglecting my wife, my plan is to make up for it during conjugal visits. Alia is so little that she'll sleep through most of the two days. The first thing I do once I'm classified is submit an application. It comes back two weeks later stating I have no proof of marriage— even though we got married inside a prison. Anita has to purchase a copy of our marriage license. This takes another month. Ultimately, we're scheduled for late in November. In early November, after losing multiple hearings before the legislature, Governor Pete Wilson orders the Director of Corrections to issue an emergency administrative rule change severely curtailing the family visiting program. Victims' rights advocates have finally triumphed in their quest to shut it down. All lifers, including lifers without parole, are banned from participating. I'm disappointed but not surprised.

When I had been at Tehachapi, while I still orbited in the clerk's universe, I knew an older guy named Larry Mount. Originally from Bakersfield, he had been an oil company geologist, and was one of the few middle-class, educated white guys I've met in the joint. I never asked him why he was in, but the rumors held he had killed a business partner. His wife Tina, a beautifully quirky woman, got along well with Anita. Now he's the lead clerk at Lancaster. After some cajoling, he talks me into going back to work for the guards. I'm reluctant at first, but it's a pay number and comes with a few perks. As a clerk, in all but the most dire circumstances, you aren't ever really locked down. Because you work for the sergeants and lieutenants, the regular line guards tend to leave you alone. It's also easier to exercise some measure of control over your life. The bad part: you work directly for the guards.

My first day starts off inauspiciously. The regular sergeant, while looking directly at me from across the hall, starts bellowing, "Clerk! Clerk!" In all my years of being a clerk, no one has ever yelled for me to come. I look right back at him and yell, just as loudly, "Sergeant! Sergeant!" He gets up and storms into my office all red-faced.

You heard me.

I have a name.

I don't know your name.

I don't come when people yell. If you want me just signal me, and my name is Hartman.

He leaves, unsatisfied by this exchange. Later, Larry tells me they don't like my attitude. I don't like their attitude. This is the start of a few months of unpleasantness. The supervisors do a lot of yelling, and my fellow clerks do a lot of scurrying. It doesn't sit well. But it gets back to the immutable fact of working for the guards.

At one level, we're all working for the guards, no matter what the job assignment. If you work on the yard crew, your supervisor is a guard who tells you which piece of ground to weed, where the papers need to be picked up. If you're a building porter, the guards in the building tell you which spot on the concrete floor needs mopping. In the kitchen, the clothing room, pretty much everywhere, the guards have the final say. But being a clerk, particularly a custody clerk, puts a prisoner into a more direct and personal level of contact with them. I'm a disciplinary clerk and an incident clerk. My job is to type up the reports generated by the line guards documenting the misbehavior of my fellow prisoners. This puts me in an uncomfortable spot on both sides of the divide. Prisoners often conclude that if the clerks weren't typing the tales of their nefarious exploits, they wouldn't be suffering the consequences. Guards, too, often expect clerks to "clean up" their reports, fixing their spelling and correcting their grammar.

But there is a positive side to this proximity. Although few close relationships develop, it's natural to discover commonality and connections—similar backgrounds, compatible musical tastes and team loyalties. Add to this the simple fact of working in the same space five days a week, eight hours a day for years, and it's hard not to get to know people, even come to like them. But you aren't supposed to like a guard, and they aren't supposed to like you. It's tough to reconcile these contradictions. After I move to the night shift to get away from the hollering sergeant and the excessive kowtowing, I come to appreciate working for a couple of my supervisors. One, who shares my birthday, is a hard-edged and rough-cut Mexican sergeant, born and raised in East Los Angeles. Right away, he treats me as a human being, and extends to me all the courtesies he can. The other supervisor, older than me, I have known since he started as a guard at Tehachapi. Now a lieutenant, he is out of place in this world, too soft-spoken, too fair-minded. He tells me he left Tehachapi because of the brutality and hostility. I look forward to seeing him when I go to work.

My days are taken up with exercising on the iron pile. I try to hit the pile at least four or five times a week. Lifting weights is as much a part of prison as tattoos and bad poetry. In the last few years, there has been a growing movement to do away with weights—an unimaginable deprivation. Even the loss of conjugal visits, terrible and depressing though it is, doesn't feel as intolerable. The idea of men going out to a semi-private area and having sex, on prison grounds, has always seemed a little fanciful. It is also a relatively new option and affects a relatively small number of prisoners. The iron pile, by contrast, both feels right—like it *should be* there—and has a much wider impact. But the argument has been made that we're "paroling too big"—when guys get out, their sizes make them seem menacing to the general public. There is more than a bit of the barbarian myth to this, as if kraken and behemoth were breaking down the walls to storm the real world. At my biggest and strongest, when I could bench press more than four hundred pounds, any cop's 9-mm pistol could easily stop me.

The restrictions started with the fiction that we needed to be protected from ourselves. Too many injuries are occurring on account of the unsafe weightlifting practices we dumb prisoners employ. The prison system requires us to take a safety test, composed of basic questions anyone could pass. Even the guards know it's pointless. Next, an upper limit on the available weight is set to prevent us from achieving the massive size that renders us immune to bullets. This is equally ridiculous because it simply forces us to do more repetitions to get the desired results. As it turns out, none of these measures satisfy the get-tough crowd, who really want us to suffer in a state of bored dissipation as we reflect on the wrongs of our life.

Therefore, one warm spring day, a large flatbed truck rolls onto the yard. A group of staff begins the process of loading all the benches, the dumbbells, the bars, and the piles of quarters, dimes, and nickels. I sit on the bench outside the program office. The yard is empty; everyone is locked in their cells. Because I'm a clerk, I can be out. I feel a tremendous sense of loss. It's hard to imagine my life without my regular trips to the iron pile, which now lies in a heap in the back of a truck like a pile of junk. For weeks afterward, the denuded area has the devastated quality of a bomb crater. Occasionally, one or two guys who ordered their lives around chest days and arm days, myself included, can be seen loitering where they once sought release from the ennui of prison life. It is during this period that it becomes clear to me how far the advocates of punishment-for-the-sake-of-inflicting-pain will go to turn the clock back. The reforms I've taken for granted—personal clothes, contact visiting, the right to grow my hair and beard to whatever length I desire, the ability to write to whomever I choose—are brand new in the history of prisons in America. In my lifetime, particularly in the South, men were being tied to whipping posts and flogged at the guards' discretion. The coming years will see the loss of most of the progressive reforms won during the '70s. It is no coincidence these years will also see the rise of mass violence and the failure of more than two-thirds of parolees. Sitting on a wooden bench bolted to the wall, I see all of this coming with a clarity that proves prescient.

All the while, I'm lulled into a state of complacency by the magical weekends with my daughter. Anita has battled the prison into reopening the play area where I spend whole days rolling around on the floor with Alia. The vile woman who had created so much heartache is gone, replaced by a reasonable guard whom Alia comes to see as her friend. Determined not to poison her with the racial hatred I grew up with, I take great pains to introduce her to my black friends. Nor do I want her to see the guards as her enemy, so I encourage her to speak with them, too. Whenever she sees the visiting room officer, she runs to him and gives him a tiny little hug. It's an awkward and beautiful moment.

As it turns out, sadly, most of my fellow prisoners can't turn off the prison act while in the visiting room. Getting down on the floor on your hands and knees violates the macho posture of the prison yard. I don't imagine I could have done it when I was younger; I was too riddled with self-conscious doubts and fears. The upshot is that I become the de facto babysitter in the play area. One time, the sergeant, lieutenant, and administrators stop in the visiting room to marvel at the sight: four, five, sometimes more kids of all shades and hues, and one 235-pound white convict with a shaved head engaged in the games of childhood. Wrestling, reading stories from books where I adopt numerous voices and guises, and, best of all, building things out of Lego blocks.

We call our constructions "guys"—one of my favorite words for everybody. Whenever Alia comes to visit, we build some guys. Our favorite guys are "jet-dogs," which we make out of differently colored blocks that somehow determine their personalities and characteristics. Red and green blocks make Christmas dogs who are generous and like to give presents. They live in houses and throw parties with the other jet-dogs. Remarkably, these guys always do the same things, always have the same reactions, and never deviate from the expected script. I can see how this would grate on the average free person who's used to variety and choice. For me, it is easy to adopt a routine, which is the key to adjusting to the prison experience. Playing with the Lego guys brings me more pleasure, more joy and healing, than anything else in my life.

Every visit starts the same, with the same moment of total escape. When I come through the visiting-room door, no matter what she's doing or where she is in the room, Alia comes running to me and jumps into my arms. Each time this happens, another brick in the wall I've erected around myself over the years is dislodged. It's Alia's greatest gift: pure, unsullied, uncomplicated love wrapped around me like a protective shield.

This life of extremes, of terrible losses and inconceivable gains, is the life I lead. And I lead it in a kind of foggy semi-awareness, as if the love I'm absorbing has the magical ability to protect me when I go back through the door into the darkness of prison. I'm still working on my accounting course, the advanced portion, with lovely Demree. I see it as the closest I'll ever get to the ten years' study of mathematics Plato recommends prior to undertaking the study of philosophy, which is my ultimate goal. I want to write a dissertation on the philosophical basis underlying the practice of punishment. In that I have only a California High School Proficiency Examination, I'm a long way off from this pursuit. My ultimate goal is to teach philosophy in a small community college in some upper-middle-class, suburban city. I've had this dream for many years.

Before taking my place on the faculty of Anytown College, I want to travel the country in a converted bus. The genesis of this was a brochure that came to me when I was in the hole in Tehachapi. I have no idea how I ended up on their mailing list, but a Canadian company that does custom conversions sent me a full-color sampling of this product. For a long-term prisoner, used to living in a space smaller than the average bathroom, a forty-five-foot bus is enormous. And I like the idea of being able to take my house on the road.

My concrete home, rooted firmly in the high desert's alkali soil, is harder to bear with conjugal visits gone, the iron pile gone, and more restrictions on the way. Now that I'm a clerk, I've moved to a cell that's at least marginally quieter, so I try to meditate as often as I can. Usually, the boom boxes are silenced in the early morning hours before breakfast. I have also joined the Native American Spiritual Circle here, so I go out to the sweat lodge area most Saturday mornings until Anita arrives. I meet a wonderful Buddhist monk named Kshanti, a supremely intelligent and compassionate woman who becomes a mentor and friend to both Anita and me. She comes to the prison as a religious volunteer, and I spend a couple of years attending meditation classes under her guidance. I learn a tremendous amount, but I can never accept the cosmology of Buddhism. It becomes clear to me that I need a more structured approach to spirituality, a more assertive approach to tackling life. I even consider returning to the religion of my youth, Catholicism, a supremely structured system. I'm seeking peace inside my heart—a method of attaining and maintaining peace, a *way*.

The revelation finally comes to me: What is happening around me is wrong. The way the staff is allowing the violence and disorder, the way some of them encourage it, is wrong. The way my fellow prisoners have been hypnotized by racial politics, by the mad pursuit of drugs, by their allegiance to this code of conduct that demands violence, and by our complete failure to stand up and take back our dignity—it is all wrong. I seek in the religious experience an escape from the world of prison, a way to complete my inward turn and remove myself from its terrible anarchy. But I cannot.

The inculcation of that code within me is too deep. My only alternative is to change this world by transforming the meaning of the code's strictures. Turn it inside out. Take what has become a way to justify the demonstrably wrong and reformulate it as the basis for a radically transformative experience.

I can remember sitting in the office with an old Mexican lieutenant who goes all the way back to San Quentin. Both of us are reading the same signals. The takeaways, the restrictions, the overcrowding are leading to inevitable tragedy. On the yard, I talk with several of my fellow older prisoners and come to the same conclusion: there is a storm coming, and it will reach our yard eventually unless we can figure out how to erect a barrier strong enough to resist the disruption. None of us, prisoners or guards, are seers. This storm has already begun to engulf Mother California's harsher outposts. Riots, the ultimate scourge of a prison, when all hell breaks loose and the rule of law disappears in a mass of unrestrained violence—this is the new paradigm.

I'm sitting in the lieutenant's office. It's late at night and I'm working on an incident report. This prison system, a calamity surrounded by gun towers, loves its forms. Everything that happens is recorded in one form or another, usually typed by prisoner-clerks. Lieutenant Foster—a man who looks like a young Billy Dee Williams, the suave black actor of the '60s and '70s, and has a voice far too soft and calm for this world—and I are bemoaning the course of things. It's our usual conversation, one I imagine is taking place between veteran lieutenants and veteran prisoners all across the state. At some point, I suggest we need to create a yard for those of us who simply want to do our time, away from the bullshit and the madness.

Well, Hartman, you put something together and I'll take it to the warden.

You know it would die in the chain of command.

I eat lunch with Ernie Roe every week. It can't be coming from an inmate. Do it under my name.

For the next few weeks, I talk with several of my closest friends, and I talk with the guards I work for, seeking to come up with a plan that could actually work. Initially, the plan is to use a minimum-age criterion, but I fear there are too few older guys, and I have to admit not every younger guy is as much of an idiot as I was. There has to be an incentive for the prison to transform an entire facility, so I focus on Facility-A, which has all of the vital services, the main kitchen, the central laundry facility, the plant operations shops that fix the broken pipes and the faulty wires. These have been regularly disrupted by all the lockdowns, and the lockdowns have created the opening needed to give this venture at least a chance of success. What I've sensed in all the many conversations I've had with the staff while typing up incident reports is a sense of fatigue on their end. Riots, work strikes, sit-down strikes, the deluge of paperwork have worn them out. The promise of a stable yard where they can perform their essential functions, at least one place in the prison that isn't a misspoken word away from meltdown, is appealing.

It isn't hard to put together a criterion for prisoners based on a minimum amount of time served, time free of disciplinary problems, and a willingness to abide by the basic rules. Of course, because we all understand the devastating impact of drugs, there has to be a serious attempt to suppress demand through regular, compulsory testing. (Supply cannot be stopped.) Finally, those who are actively involved with prison gangs have to be excluded. (They would, most likely, exclude themselves.) None of this is tough to come up with. I know exactly who needs to be barred from this experiment: me, or me of fifteen years ago. I know this because I wouldn't want to do time with that person, not now.

We need a name that reflects what is possible, that speaks to a higher purpose and provides the aspirational element we all hope for as a way out of the downward spiral. I settle on the Honor Yard Program, which both reaches back into the history of California prisons and asks for something more out of the men. In what seems like a long time ago, there were honor dorms and blocks at many institutions. This was before the system decided that every prisoner had forfeited his claim to humanity when he arrived at the gate, before society had concluded we were all a contagion in need of containment behind hermetically sealed walls and lethal fences. The name is also evocative of the desire that all men be better than their worst act, to surmount the tyranny of low expectations we labor under.

The final proposal is a compact, eight-page blueprint for how to convert a single, six-hundred-man facility into a functional yard. Lieutenant Foster takes it to his lunch with Warden Roe, a man who's not of the suppression school. He was a teacher in prison prior to moving up the ranks. At Tehachapi, when the guards tried to bar Anita for complaining too much and too loudly, he took the unheard of step of meeting with her directly and reinstating her visiting privileges. A substantial man with a rare talent for being able to speak with everyone, he asks after my wife whenever he sees me. To his credit, he recognizes the possibilities of the Honor Yard Program right away. He assigns the newly arrived Catholic priest, a deeply educated man, to develop and refine the proposal, along with a sharp captain who was also at Tehachapi. The culture of failure at Lancaster is so entrenched that new ideas have to come from outside.

As the months go by and it becomes clear this program has a real chance of being implemented, the identity of the author gets around. The fact that a prisoner came up with this fundamental shift in direction is bitterly resented by many of the staff. As more time goes by, a lot of other people will claim ownership of the idea, proving the old adage about success having many fathers. I work with the priest, behind the scenes, and help to keep him focused on the prisoners' side of the project. It's vital to remind him, and pretty much all the rest of the staff, that without the prisoners' agreement to support this program, or any other, it won't succeed. He knows a great deal about the meaning of honor, what the restoration of a man entails, and his Irish brogue and white collar add gravity to the cause. In late 2000, while the prison is still managing one catastrophe after another, Warden Roe initiates the transition of Facility-A into the Honor Yard Program. Prisoners and staff will be held to a higher standard. Expectations will shift from failure to success. The reigning ethos of prison, which is punishment for the sake of inflicting pain, will be replaced with something more humane, something more positive. It is a quiet revolution, but real.

*

For me, as momentous and satisfying a victory as all this is, my personal life has gone in the opposite direction and come undone.

Anita decides to breastfeed Alia until the baby stops of her own accord, which turns out to be right after her third birthday, in early '99. Over the past year, Anita has become increasingly frustrated by everything. She tried going back to a normal job, but couldn't readjust to the working life. For two years, she has lived off her savings and unemployment and the generosity of her family. During this time, she has become increasingly bitter and hostile. She engages in battles with the guards every weekend, and I'm forced into playing referee. When I point out what a great blessing it is to have a healthy child, a decent place to live, and a family willing to help her out, she reacts like I've thrown acid on her face. Our visits degenerate into fights and accusations, followed by her threats to divorce me.

It's heartbreaking to see the devastating impact this has on little Alia. Like every child, she wants her parents to get along. One of the worst moments of my life is when she puts her hands over our mouths and says, "Stop fighting!" No child should ever have to say those words.

Every weekend Anita seems more wound up. One day I come into the visiting room and find her talking to herself. She's obsessed with some dark, repressed memory that she feels guilty about, but she won't tell me what it is. I begin to suspect she had an affair early on in our marriage and is now suffering remorse. When I confront her, she confirms my suspicion and confesses that it was with someone we both know. I'm crushed, but I conclude that what's done is done. We move on.

My mother-in-law, Emma, is watching Alia for a couple of days while Anita is away. I call the day she's supposed to get back, but Emma is evasive. She tells me there was some trouble, but that she'll be back tomorrow. When I finally talk to Anita, she sounds different, altered in such a profound way that I'm not even sure it's Anita on the phone. Her voice is flat and barely audible. She tells me she ended up wandering around Sacramento, smoking Camels and hearing voices, then walked out into the street and lay down in traffic. I ask her why, but she says she can't tell me. There is a monotone quality to her speech, as if something inside of her is broken. The past months have been tough, and I feel drained from all the fighting. It has been more than three years since we were together for a family visit. No one expects conjugal visits to ever return, and Anita has told me so many times that it's a hated refrain, I can't go on forever without sex. Part of me wants to throw in the towel right then and move on. I have so much stress on me, living in a war zone, trying to navigate around the obstacles of my fellow prisoners while I work to create something better.

Anita came to my rescue when I was lost. She shepherded me back from my self-exile and into a communion that I never knew existed. Now, with the thorn of my rage removed, I feel indebted to her in ways too profound to leave her lying in a street somewhere. And deeper still, more elementally, there is the question of Alia. No one can doubt how much she loves her dad, and no one who knows me can doubt how much I love my daughter. She is the embodiment of all I dream and hope for; she is innocence and possibility in a life, literally, without possibility. I manage to convince Anita to come by herself, so we can talk.

It's Friday, a visiting day, and I'm standing in front of my wife. Or at least she looks like my wife, but this poor broken creature cannot be Anita. She's agitated and jumps at the slightest sound. When I ask her to tell me what happened, she gives me vague answers, blaming the cigarettes for her unusual behavior, but she doesn't smoke, and never has. She tells me her hormones are all messed up because she's turning forty. She mumbles on, not making sense. But the words are the least of it. She walks differently, tentatively, without the purposeful stride I'm used to seeing. Her voice is weaker than ever. Can this be the woman who took singing lessons for so many years, who is loud enough to stop a prison visiting room, to shout me down?

It's what is missing from her eyes, though, that is most troubling. The sensate glow, the inner luminescence that makes her human, is gone. It's not just dimmed or diminished; it is gone. Later, when I'm describing her condition to a friend, I will say that something inside of her broke; what I really want to say is that something inside her is dead. How can the person she was be resurrected? I despair for Alia. And I remember my own mother. Something inside of her had died, too, and it must have happened before I was conscious.

*

The facility I live on has begun to implode, but I'm so distracted by my own travails I miss the moment. At the heart of the meltdown are two of the most combustible factors in the joint: race and drugs. The prison system is scamming money out of the federal government by creating Potemkin village drug abuse programs. The only things these programs appear to accomplish is to concentrate a couple of hundred dope fiends into one housing unit and make it easy to know where to score. A high percentage of the heroin addicts are white guys, while the heroin trade on this yard is controlled by the Mexicans. This creates an unsustainable tension: white guys going deeper and deeper into debt, a debt they don't have the ability to pay, to members of a group superior in numbers and organization.

Most mornings when we're not locked down, I go out to the yard, oblivious to what's going on, and do some pull-ups, push-ups, and handstands. I jog a couple of miles if my knees feel up to it. The group of us that's not on drugs is a dwindling percentage of the population. The lure of release through the abyss of bliss is sucking in more guys every day. It has reached such epidemic proportions that I see little knots on the yard passing around hot rigs—unsterilized needles. It does little good to counsel against sharing needles because the fear of despair outweighs the fear of disease. I remember how I refused to heed the warnings of older prisoners when I was caught in the well, and this was years before the out-front "screw you" mentality of the youngest prisoners took over the system. Over the past few months, there have been minor skirmishes between the slow-paying users and the dealers' enforcers. Each time, the pressure is ratcheted up a notch. The latest group of penny-ante shot-callers have taken to passing a collection plate around to extort the funds needed to pay for their habits. I refuse to contribute.

It's a warm, windy, early summer morning. I'm at the front of the yard, directly under the observation tower, doing pull-ups, talking with a couple of guys. There have been persistent rumors of white dopers and Mexican dope dealers preparing for conflict. The yard is split down the middle by an eight-foot-tall chain-link fence. The trouble seems to be on the other side, emanating from the drug treatment building. I notice a ripple of quick movement behind me. As I turn toward the other yard, it looks like a school of blue-clad fish churning out from a central spot in the grass. The yard alarm sounds its wailing pitch. Down on the yard! Down on the yard! This routine isn't at all out of the ordinary; we hear it almost every day. I start to turn back toward my yard to sit down when I see one of my closest Mexican friends jump up and start running toward the back of the yard. He is yelling wildly: It's on with the whites, let's go!

In the next few minutes, the Mexicans on the yard, close to a hundred, leap to their feet as one mass and run toward the small grass area in front of the showers. Simultaneously, all the Mexicans on the other yard do the same, heading to a point of convergence. There are four of us at the bars. Since the outbreak of mass riots a couple of years ago, I have rehearsed in my mind what I would do at a moment like this. Circle up! We are standing, back-to-back, in a rough circle. I see a white guy out on the field in a savage dance with a couple of Mexican nationals. Get over here! The area in front of the grass is a scrum. I can see the flash of knives, hear the screams and growls of men lost to the adrenaline of combat. Staying about ten yards from our position are about a dozen Mexican nationals who clearly have no great desire to rush us any more than we have to rush them.

In the scenarios I played out imagining this eventuality, the overwhelming force of the guards quelled the riot almost immediately. The reality is the guards have run off the yard and hidden behind the protection of the fences, leaving us—outnumbered five to one—to our fate. The observation tower has lobbed in a dozen tear gas pellets, but in the ever-present wind they're completely ineffective. They look like the smoke pots we used to throw during Fourth of July celebrations, and have the same level of deterrent impact. It's clear to me the guards have surrendered the yard to the gangs, and once surrendered, it will be extremely difficult for them to retake. By the time the guards reenter the yard, the fighting and stabbing is long over, all fury spent. As we're being placed in plastic flex-cuffs, I look over to see one of my Mexican friends. Our eyes meet and he shakes his head before looking back down.

The effect of this riot on the facility is profound. For a California prison yard to function there are several unspoken but agreed upon propositions. First among these is the idea that order will be maintained, and this means order within our own ranks. There are occasions, every day, where the groups are disproportionate in size. It's not uncommon for a dozen people sitting in a holding tank—waiting for the doctor, in the library, or locked in a sally port waiting for the yard end to open—to be eleven of one group and one of another. There is an assumption that we prisoners would never take advantage of this imbalance: it would be dishonorable. Similarly, there is an assumption that the guards will keep order in the event of a riot, or regain it quickly. They have all the advantages, from rifles to communications to plans and training. In fact, they train all the time. This time, we prisoners abdicated our humanity, and the guards abdicated their responsibility, failing in our most basic functions, all of us. Up until this moment, I have never seen a yard completely disintegrate. The stories had always seemed more than a little exaggerated, but now I have seen it with my own eyes. It's worse than I feared, much worse. The prison has truly come undone.

We are on lockdown, a complete lockdown that will last for months. This is the functional equivalent of the guards throwing up their hands and walking off the field. For me, it means no time out of my cell for weeks, and I only get out early because I'm a privileged clerk. Showering is a birdbath in the sink. Food comes on paper trays, in much smaller portions, cold and congealed. There is no access to the canteen. There is no access to religious services. Visiting is shut down. This means the sense of disempowered rage and impotent frustration that simmers at the core of the prison experience is crammed back into the cells. Nothing good ever comes of this, not in all my years in Mother California's institutions. The only certain outcome is that men are reduced to animals trapped in a cage.

The effect of all this on me is equally profound. Too many traumatic events in too little time. Throughout all my many years behind bars, even in juvenile hall, I have been close to the Mexicans. There has never been a moment when I've felt uncomfortable around them. I have always respected their loyalty and generosity. With this turn of events, a substantial number of my friends can no longer be my friends. It's a matter of personal safety.

I'm also furious with the addicts whose failure to abide by one of the most basic tenets of prison life—pay your debts—has dragged us all down. Of course, the addicts are equally furious with me. The new perspective in prison, one I refuse to subscribe to, is that we are all draftees into the army led by a few face-tattooed losers who've served a whole five years, and who claim to have the "keys" to the yard granted by a mythical roundtable up north. Whenever one of them gets into a jam, we all have to march into battle under their direction. Not for me, this abjuring of personal autonomy. These guys believe everyone on the yard should have to run through the blasts of 30-mm block gunfire to join them in getting mopped in the grass.

*

The Honor Yard Program is in the final stages of implementation. The warden has green-lighted the transition. In about six months, the first volunteers should be moving over to Facility-A. In the meantime, this facility is over and done. After so explosive an event as a mass race riot, prisoners regress into a primitive tribalism that boils down to rage and fear and revenge. For the first couple of weeks after that dreadful day, the angry buzz is all about revenge. To avenge the honor of our fellow white men, we must go out to the yard and stab Mexicans. That none of the Mexicans who stabbed whites are on the yard isn't relevant, and neither is the simple fact that most of these Mexicans were compelled to act out of fear of retaliation by their own army commanders. I get a few kites from my Mexican friends, apologizing and explaining that they had no choice. The whole affair is disastrous for everyone involved. I decide to pull my clerk juice—resign my privileged job—and move to Housing Unit #1, the mental health program building. I get a single cell and a measure of peace.

Anita is doing a bit better. She's still bringing Alia most weekends. The worst manifestations of her collapse have waned. She writes it off as an aberration, and claims not to need the help of a shrink. What concerns me is Alia. She says strange things in the innocent and open manner of children. Mommy is acting weird. Mommy sleeps all the time. I talk with everyone I know, but no one offers me any useful advice. The most common suggestion is that Anita should be seeing a shrink. There is no way I can make this happen, even if Anita consented to go. How would I pay for it?

When the first group selected for the Honor Yard is moved to Facility-A, I'm not in it. I could have been, but the lieutenant and sergeant I've worked for all these years convince me to lay back and see what happens over the next few months. Many guards and prisoners believe the Honor Yard will detonate, along with the whole concept. I myself wonder if this might happen. The current residents are being pushed out, and no prisoner likes to be pushed. Facility-A has been notorious throughout the institution. There have been several major riots in the past couple of years. One of the housing units is known as "Thunderdome" for obvious reasons. The dope is flowing freely. The guards have resigned themselves to standing at the edges of the yard, watching the violent drama unfold. Because of all the incident reports I have typed that came off Facility-A, none of this is news to me. And there's another obstacle: the various shot-callers have decreed that anyone in good standing must refuse to participate. They are the first group, understandably, to see how this program could transform our world. Motivated by negative intentions though they may be, these prisoners are cunning and grasp the dynamics of the prison world in ways few guards ever do.

A surprising thing happens as the conversion takes place: nothing. In a few short weeks, a couple of months all told, Facility-A is a different place. The quiet is unnerving to all accustomed to the raging din. Guards who work overtime shifts tell me they're shocked. The recalcitrant prisoners just left, without a fight, and the reactionary guards who are used to daily affirmation of their power find themselves railing against the peace. The priest tells me I'm missing an opportunity I helped to create. It is time to move.

But I don't want to move. Or rather, I don't want to leave the unique little haven I have carved out for myself. I have my own single cell, which is so relaxing. The days of bonding with a cellie—of doing group time, playing cards, feeling like I'm part of a team—are over. The years have burned all of that out of me. I like being by myself. I also have a good job with decent bosses. They're guards, to be sure, but I have known them now for years. I feel comfortable around them, and they feel the same way. This comfort factor is why the rules were changed to make it impossible for a clerk to hold the same job for more than a year—they call it the "overfamiliarity rule." To beat this, I swap with another guy every year so it appears I'm not always a clerk, but this is on paper only. Throughout the institution, there are familiarity police, or "haters" as they're often called. It's easy to forget how much these guards detest the idea of prisoners as men instead of inmates. Every night when I go to work, I go back to the lieutenant's office and make a fresh pot of coffee. It's part of my routine. A good cup and a smoke, because I smoke again.

The night I finally leave for the Honor Yard is cold and windy. I've said my good-byes. I'm standing at the gate with my worldly goods packed into a big laundry cart. The beautiful Filipino guard—who makes me understand why my father always spoke with such longing for the Philippines—looks at me with the eyes of a woman who knows me. "You're sad to be leaving. That's so sweet. We'll miss you." I'll miss her, too.

The radio crackles: the count is clear. She puts the handcuffs on in front so I can push the cart over to Facility-A.

California State Prison, Los Angeles County: II

A few weeks of living here and I'm worn out from all the yard time. During the past couple of years, I felt lucky to get outside a couple of times a week for an hour. This yard runs all day, every day. It is a common observation I hear from all the new arrivals. The white guys look sunburned; we had become ghosts. The other aspect of my fellow prisoners I notice right off is how fat and healthy everyone looks. Years of stress and fear masquerading as rage whittled us down to the negative sum of our existence. In just the past few months, some of the guys who first came over have acquired a kind of inner ease; the haunted look in their eyes is gone. Across the yard, I see men engaged in different pursuits. One group is sitting in a circle praying, another is kicking around a Hacky Sack, others are rapping together with great, joyful zest. The armed encampments of a maximum-security yard have vanished. I see blacks, whites, and Latinos standing next to each other without the stiff shoulders and rapid glances that characterize the so-called active yard. On one of my first days outside, I see an apparently sane prisoner sleeping on the grass.

After a couple of months of leisure, I take a job as a clerk during the day. The process of taking the program beyond a basic yard largely free of violence requires access to the locus of power. It also requires finding a way to bypass the elected representatives of the prisoners, the Men's Advisory Council, universally known by the acronym MAC. In my experience, MACs are all the same: pandering, demagogic, manipulative, and self-serving groups that seek to enrich themselves at the expense of their putative constituents. In California prisons—the only place in modern America where this could happen—we elect representatives by race. The blacks vote for blacks, the whites for whites, the Latinos for Latinos, the others for others. It's the law of the land.

I start with the Honor Program Committee, but the staff is determined to lay claim to that name. Most employees of the prison system don't believe we're capable of managing ourselves. It's necessary for them to hold this belief in order to justify their own authority. I settle on the Steering Committee for the Honor Program. I handpick a select group of men who are all veterans; who have intelligence and skills; and who have a deep commitment to foundational transformation. This group is also racially representative. Nothing will motivate prisoners against each other more than the belief that one race is somehow getting over on another. I sit down with the current MAC chairman, a sincere and diligent Black Muslim, and explain my agenda and intentions. I want to organize a shadow group that will go about the business of realizing our vision of the Honor Program. The MAC spends its energies focused on immediate, short-term issues: the yard was late yesterday, or the canteen should sell more candy bars. We prisoners need a group of elders to consider the long-term focus: to provide a map for the road we'll need to travel down in order to find our place in the human community.

*

Just at this point, as I'm feeling the pressure of responsibility for the ambitious project I've set in motion, Anita undergoes a stunning and frightening deterioration. She visits less frequently, and when she does come, she gets here at the end of the day. The light in her eyes, which had begun to flicker back on, dims again. She is so distracted that I have to wave a hand in front of her face to bring her back. Anita's family is concerned about little Alia's welfare. It takes me too long to recognize the gravity of the situation, and once I do, I'm knocked down by despair. I'm confronted by the reality of my situation, and the vulnerability of the innocent being I helped bring into this world. In all my years of imprisonment, no matter the circumstances, irrational though it may have been, I always felt like I retained the power to affect the outcome. This situation is entirely different. I am powerless. I am impotent. My perfect little girl, who loves me more than I probably deserve, is imperiled, and I can do nothing.

For weeks, our only contact is through phone calls. Fifteen minutes of madness interspersed by the purity of a child.

How are you doing Anita?

I don't have anything to say to you.

Can I talk to Alia?

The phone hits something hard, a resounding "thunk" in my ears. I hear Anita shrieking to Alia that I'm on the phone. Alia picks up.

Hi Daddy.

Hey kitty cat, how are you?

I'm okay.

Is everything all right?

She pauses, and then lies, telling me that everything's okay. It breaks my heart to hear her lie to cover for her mother. Sometimes I call and Alia answers and accepts the charges. When I ask her where her mother is, she tells me she's in the bathtub, Anita spends hours in the tub. Alia watches movies on television. They live up in a semi-isolated area near a manmade lake, not far from the prison. Some of their neighbors have horses and chickens. I worry about the isolation.

All these years, Anita's family and I have never established any serious ties. I am the convict who stole away an innocent girl. For a long time, I resented them, but during the years of my awakening it dawned on me that they were only trying to protect her. Now that I have a daughter, I understand them better. I wouldn't want Alia to end up with who I was then, or even who I am now, trapped in a snare of permanent separation. For the sake of my daughter, I reach out to Anita's parents, Bill and Emma. Alia is their relative, too.

When Anita lay down on the street in Sacramento, she swore me to secrecy. She told her parents she had been attacked and mugged, which explained her shell-shocked condition. I write to my mother-in-law and reveal what actually happened. Emma begins making clandestine trips up to the lake house. What she discovers horrifies me. Anita and Alia are living in a messy, disordered nightmare of a house. It's worse than I ever imagined.

For the last time in my life, I write my parents and ask for the addresses of my younger brother and sister. I receive no reply. I ask a friend to pay for an Internet search, which turns up nothing except that my father may have died recently. I ask the priest to call my mother to try to get my brother's address. In all these years, I've only had a few contacts with either of my younger siblings. Early at Tehachapi, my younger sister intercepted one of my irregular letters to my parents and responded. She was seeing a guy who found it odd that she never saw me. I sent her a visiting application, but while it was being processed she dropped out of sight again. At some other point, Anita spoke with my younger brother and set up a meeting. For reasons unclear, the meeting never happened. On another occasion, long before Alia was born, Anita drove down to Northtown, determined to heal our rift. After a few minutes of tense conversation at the door I once kicked to the ground on Harding Street, the police showed up and asked her to leave.

I give the priest the phone number. He dials and catches my mother. I leave his office and wait in the hallway; it's disquieting to know that my mother is only inches away from me. He speaks to her for a long time, much longer than I would have expected. After he gets off the phone, he calls me back into his office. That is the most depressing woman I've ever talked to, he tells me with real compassion in his eyes and weariness in his voice. No addresses are forthcoming. I will not be able to call on my family to help my daughter. In light of our family history, I'm not overly surprised.

Somehow, Anita manages to get herself banned from visiting me. Over the past year, her warfare with the guards has escalated. I spend a good part of the week fielding hostile shots from one or another guard she has offended. But the rules require Anita to bring Alia in herself or officially approve someone else. I have no say in the matter. My daughter proves to be a tenacious combatant herself and goads her mother into allowing others to bring her to visit. My mother-in-law and my ever loyal and amazing friend Linda take on the job. Even so, it is such a sad and reduced experience to sit in the visiting room with our daughter, without her mother, my wife.

*

The Honor Program is taking shape. The simple set of rules allows for a space of peace to be created. We press for community service projects, groups to counsel wayward youth, seedlings growing to reforest the fire-ravaged hillsides of burned-down California. We hope to train service dogs for the disabled in our cells. Fundamentally, we desire to transform Mother California prisons by giving ourselves the chance to become useful citizens instead of common criminals.

It soon becomes obvious to all that our high-functioning yard presents a direct challenge to the get-tough party line that has been used to justify the years of takeaway management. The safety and security mantra, the holy writ of prison, gets invoked with a vengeance at the first sign of any challenge to the status quo. For reasons of safety and security, we must not be allowed conjugal visits, weights, personal clothing, long hair, more than ten books, or the ability to communicate with the media. As the actual safety and security deteriorate with the increased number of restrictions, a curious fallacy of reasoning takes hold: the failure of the tougher rules to bring order demand still tougher rules.

Within the system, there's no motive for change. Its constituent parts—the administrators, the managers, the guards, the shrinks, the maintenance people, the teachers, and the vast infrastructure of suppliers—have all profited from the way things are done. Few see any reason to change. Lucky for us, like any massive entity, Mother California fails to see the threat of something as innocuous as the Honor Program until we've gained a small purchase on the real estate. Once it does, the reprisals and sabotage begin in earnest. None of it is very creative, just the usual fomenting of violence that's as much a part of prison life as loneliness and remorse. It's a tactic that has always worked before. But the powers that be have failed to account for a couple of factors. This yard is heavy with guys a lot like me: older, serving forever, and tired of the pointless drama of the average prison yard. We've all seen friends stabbed for no reason, brutality that has no cause. We're beyond provocation. The Honor Yard works.

The disrupters also fail to account for the warden's daughter. I'm working in the program office as a clerk when I hear she's coming over to our yard to be the head caseworker. Fashion-model thin, too tall, too blond, too pissed, she's a tough customer, a second-generation guard who's too steeped in the system to sympathize with what we're trying to do. Or so I think. After she settles into her office, I sit down to pitch the Honor Program to her. It doesn't go well. Her father was a warden, and she has a loyalty to the system that's hard to shake, a desire to believe that these men she has known all her life want to do the right thing. (And some of them do.) But she has a soft spot; she's somehow able to empathize with us better than any guard I've ever known.

She also has a touch of the arrogance common to people of exceptional good looks and powerful connections. Winning her to our side would provide us with a formidable ally. I'm drawn to her and feel an unlikely kinship, a deep connection that seems wholly natural despite the dense thicket of prohibitions between us. In any other world, I would pursue her, chase down these feelings and discover how it is I feel lighter around her, learn why she knows me so well and brings out the parts of me I like the most. I can't explain any of these things, not even know.

Over a period of weeks, I continue to press her.

I tell her that she's the gatekeeper, the head counselor. I tell her that she decides who comes to this program. This is a chance to do the right thing. The evidence, the fact of the improbably well-run yard right down the hall, just on the other side of the chain-link fence, cannot be denied.

The breakthrough comes when she starts referring to the yard as "our program" and makes the conceptual leap to figuring out how to instill a sense of ownership in the men. She becomes our primary patron. For the first time in this process, I have a true ally on the other side of the divide.

Next to show up is the biker captain. Not the hairy, beer-bellied kind of biker, but the dirt-track racer type. I have known this man since he was an officer and he tricked me out of my illegal cigarette lighter back at Tehachapi. He's shrewd and ambitious, and willing to fool my expectations. Although he's only an acting captain, right off he displays a fearless, almost reckless fortitude. He needs it: the blowback has already started. We speak daily, and I gently encourage him, just as I did with the warden's daughter: This is your chance to do the right thing, to make a difference. Before long, he, too, gets it.

The three of us are sitting in the captain's office. He has the back wall painted a specific orange color that matches the motorcycle brand he races. She has photos of her children and classic rock CDs on her desk. He has racing plaques all around. It's reassuring to know that people who work in here have passions much like ours. It occurs to me that we're all about the same age, and we've all been dealing with the prison system for about the same number of years. We're discussing how to advance the program. One by one, we go through a series of ideas for implementation. It's a professional meeting, not unlike what I would imagine occurs in companies and government offices every working day. There is the cordiality of collegial friendship; we all like and respect one another. As we're about to run out of topics, I toss out a few more suggestions. I don't want this moment ever to end.

Afterword

We are on lockdown, again. It's been a couple of weeks now since the latest batch of cell phones were discovered. The mass searches are in process, teams of guards moving down the tier, cell by cell, a trail of torn papers and broken property in their wake. Radios are blaring out at full volume. Shouts careen around the building, and the occasional frustrated door-kick is heard booming out in impotent rage.

It's seven years from that moment I hoped would never end. But end it did, and I am the only one of the three participants still around here, still trying to keep the Honor Program afloat.

In the past several years, whatever internal support existed has evaporated, crushed under the weight of too many things wrong in Mother California's prisons: too many prisoners serving too much time costing too much money in a time of too little resources. The prison system's leadership in the state capital has changed multiple times in a series of angry resignations.

The Honor Program became a thorn in the side of the group that ultimately runs the system, the careerists who always seem to outlast the newest reform-minded boss. The very name, implying that somehow prisoners could warrant honorable treatment or achieve honor in their lives, never sat well with this group. The chaos gave them an excuse to transfer us all out to other prisons.

The first attempt to move us was thwarted by a letter-writing campaign I organized that brought a progressive state senator named Gloria Romero to rescue the program. I spent a couple of weeks in the hole consequent to that effort.

The second attempt, a couple of years later, was met with a much more sophisticated resistance that I also led. This resulted in a bill being introduced in the state legislature that passed both houses by wide margins. Senate Bill 299 (Honor Programs Romero) would have mandated the prison system to implement the program throughout the state. The bill was supported by all the usual liberal groups, but also by the guards' union, the frontline supervisors' union, and the prison teachers' union. The crime victims' groups did not oppose it. In fact, only the upper-level administrators, the ones who simply cannot swallow the concept of "honorable prisoners," opposed the bill. Ultimately, Governor Arnold Schwarzenegger vetoed it at their behest, while promising to support its ideals. I spent another couple of weeks in the hole consequent to this effort.

During this whole process, I organized our free-world supporters into a potent force for prison reform. We established a website (www.prisonhonorprogram.org) and made connections with people of influence. Local community groups, family members, friends, and politicians volunteered to participate in what became a movement for change.

Our various prisoner groups kept striving to do good, to move out beyond the fences and into the free world, at least with their charity. Many at-risk youngsters were counseled, many pieces of artwork were auctioned off to help local nonprofits, and many prisoners were educated by their fellow prisoners.

Most gratifying and moving to me, hundreds of prisoners refused to surrender to the normal ugliness of prison and continued to work for positive change. This is the real goal of the Honor Program—the personal transformation of prisoners.

In the past few months, after a long campaign spearheaded by one of our most committed supporters, the latest prison boss came to meet with us and discuss the fate of the Honor Program. I gave a thirty-minute presentation that detailed all we had accomplished over the past eight years. He seemed impressed and promised to seriously consider actual implementation. The local officials voiced support, and the group of line guards in attendance spoke eloquently about how they, too, wanted to see the program supported. It was a love feast of common interest. Unfortunately, within weeks of the meeting, many of the programs I touted were summarily cancelled.

This lockdown looks to go on for another week or two. The administration seems particularly peeved. The state legislature is set to make bringing cell phones into prison a felony. One employee allegedly made $100,000 smuggling them into a prison up north. In the illogic of prison managers, all six hundred of us are being punished for the handful that wanted a cell phone.

I have not seen Anita or Alia for a month.

Anita is working and has recovered to a large degree. But the vibrant woman I fell in love with, who pulled me out of my downward spiral, never returned. I miss her desperately.

Alia is a teenager. She is smart and sarcastic, worldly-wise beyond her years, and possessed of a stubbornness I recognize all too well. She still looks very much like me, and she still wants to be in constant physical contact when we visit. To date, the dreaded question has not been asked, but it's coming. I will have to explain to her what I was thinking when I brought her into this life of mine.

I love them both. They both want me out there with them. They have beautiful, irrational dreams.

For as long as I can remember, all my dreams have been about prison. This world is my world, and I am a part of it. I will never again walk in the free world. Albert Camus, in *The Myth of Sisyphus*, writes that the only serious philosophical question is between life and suicide. The past three decades of my life have answered this question in the affirmative: I have chosen to make a life out of what I brought on myself. I am, after all, a stalwart son of Mother California.

Sitting at my desk, looking out my cell window across the street at an empty set of tract houses, I can see cars driving by, the lives of my neighbors just out of reach. The red flags of the prison's shooting range flutter in the dusty high desert wind. A couple pedals by the outer perimeter on bicycles. They pass behind the gun tower and then vanish out of sight.